Drift

Drift

HOW TO DEFEAT ACCIDENTAL DRIFT IN YOUR LIFE!

Scott A Clevenger

DRIFT: How To Prevent Accidental Drift In Your Life!
Copyright © 2015 by Scott A. Clevenger

All rights reserved. No part of this book may be reproduced or transmitted in any form or by any means without written permission from the author.

ISBN-13: 9781507660591
ISBN-10: 1507660596

Scripture quotations are taken from the Holy Bible, *New International Version, NIV.* Copyright 1973, 1978, 1984, 2011 by Biblica, Inc. Used by permission of Zondervan. all rights reserved worldwide. www.zondervan.com.

Scripture quotations are taken from the Holy Bible, New Living Translation, copyright ©1996, 2004, 2007 by Tyndale House Foundation. Used by permission of Tyndale House Publishers, Inc., Carol Stream, Illinois 60188. All rights reserved.

Scripture quotations marked KJV are from the King James Version of the Bible.

Scripture taken from the NEW AMERICAN STANDARD BIBLE ®, Copyright © 1960, 1962, 1963, 1968, 1971, 1972, 1973, 1975, 1977, 1995 by The Lockman Foundation. Used by permission.

Scripture taken from The Message. Copyright © 1993, 1994, 1995, 1996, 2000, 2001, 2002. Used by permission of NavPress Publishing Group.

Dedicated To:

*My wife, Amanda.
For your daily support, the greatest
blessing in my life. The one who
continues to rescue me when I drift!*

Contents

Introduction xi

Chapter 1 Defeating The Drift: Reading Your Bible 1

Chapter 2 Defeating The Drift: Un-Learning To Pray 21

Chapter 3 Defeating The Drift: Connecting With Church 37

Chapter 4 Defeating The Drift: Connecting With Others 53

Chapter 5 Defeating The Drift: Achieving Financial Control 67

Chapter 6 Defeating The Drift: Changing Stories 85

Chapter 7 Defeating The Drift: Overcoming Hurt,
            Pain & Loss Part 1 97

Chapter 8 Defeating The Drift: Overcoming Hurt,
            Pain & Loss Part 2 109

Chapter 9 Defeating The Drift: Committing To Worship 125

Chapter 10 Defeating The Drift:
            Who You Are As A Follower 137

Closing Comments 153

Appendix A
The Proverbs Challenge 157

Appendix B
The Romans 8 Challenge ·159

Appendix C
Resources For Further Growth ·161

Acknowledgements ·163

Introduction

I love vacation!
Well, let me rephrase that. I love vacation when I get to go on a vacation that I like. Have you ever been on a vacation you didn't like? I bet you have. It's with people you don't really want to be with. The place is somewhere you'd prefer not to go. You can't wait to get back home just to take a vacation from the vacation. I know the feeling, but that's not what I'm talking about.

My favorite way to vacation is cruising. In fact, I'm finalizing the manuscript for this book while I am on a cruise. I've already eaten at the buffet on the *lido* deck. I've toured the ship and checked out the casino. (No, I didn't really do that, but I do like those machines where you insert your quarter and it slides down while you bite your lower lip hoping that your quarter will be the "one" to push hundreds of other quarters into your bucket. I've never played it. But, it looks fun). Cruising is an incredibly affordable means for vacation.

Do you like to cruise?

I love to cruise because I love to eat. I can eat whatever I want and however much I want on a cruise. (Yes, I must confess my sin for eating just a little too much!) I love to cruise because with no internet or cell phones, I'm forced to detach from my common everyday life. I love to cruise because once I'm on the boat, I am waited on hand and foot. I love to cruise.

Here's the thing about a cruise boat, though. If it were to run out of fuel in the middle of the ocean, that wouldn't exactly be a good thing. Our forward momentum would propel us onward. But eventually, that momentum will die and we'll begin to drift. Once drifting kicks in, we have no control over our direction. We have no control over our destination. We have no control over whether we will ever make it back to land.

If you've never cruised before, I don't mean to scare you. I've never been on a cruise boat that has run out of fuel. But, I can remember the news reporting in years past about a boat that broke down. Once it broke down, the result was not pretty.

My point is this. I want to cruise in style with no worries. I would prefer not to drift on a cruise boat. Unfortunately, there are many in this life who have chosen that path. Rather than cruising through life in style, they're merely drifting with no control over their direction nor where they will eventually end up in life. It doesn't take much common sense to figure out that merely drifting through life will bring about a lot more stress and worry than living with a purpose.

I want something greater for you. You deserve a greater life than one that just drifts. I want to walk you through how to obtain that life. It's not difficult. But it will require some effort and intentionality from you.

Your Biggest Move Yet!

I can remember growing up having to move a couple of times. Have you ever moved? I bet you have. Moving is no fun. Since I got married and began in ministry, we've moved seven times. Every time is stressful. The sleepless nights of packing leading up to the big move. The actual move itself. Then the sleepless nights of unpacking afterwards. (And something always breaks. It's always my fault!) It's a big step to move. New job. New house. New community. New friends. New life! I'm guessing you've probably moved once or twice in your lifetime.

The move you've just taken, though, is literally towards a new life. That may not make any sense to you right now, but hopefully it will by the time you finish this book. Whether this is the first time you've ever taken a step towards God, or maybe you're trying to grow deeper, this is a big move. I want you to know that I'm excited and honored to travel on this journey with you. The Apostle Paul wrote to the Church of Corinth and said...

> *This means that anyone who belongs to Christ has become a new person. The old life is gone; a new life has begun!* (2 Cor. 5:17)

In other words, you've intentionally set your direction rather than allowing yourself to drift!

Did you notice the word "anyone." You need to know that is an all-inclusive word. If you've taken the step to accept Christ as your personal Lord and Savior, then that passage is written to you! If you've taken the step to rededicate your life to Christ, that promise is for you. You are a new person! This decision is the single greatest decision you've ever made or ever will make in your entire life. God created you with a purpose. He created you to be significant and to make a significant difference in this world.

Significance Re-Defined...

When you hear the word "significant," who comes to mind? Maybe Mother Teresa who poured out her heart to serve those less fortunate than many. Maybe you think of Billy Graham who traveled all around the world holding crusades for Christ. Maybe a Nobel Peace Prize winner comes to mind.

Here's the hurdle, though. Throughout our current American culture, we've gotten significance turned upside down. In fact, here's the myth. Most in our society would define significance as...

MYTH:
Significance = POSSESSIONS + POWER + POSITION

In other words, the more material things you can obtain the more significant you will be. But you know as well as I do that owning the newest car, the biggest house, or the latest smartphone will hardly make you significant. Those things might get you a little attention, but they won't make you significant.

Our culture believes that if you hold the power then you'll be significant. I would actually agree that if you hold power, there very well may be potential for significance. However, if you use that power in the wrong way then it surely will not be a positive significance you'll make.

Our culture also believes that the position you hold will make you significant. Again, I believe the position in which you find yourself very well might hold potential for you to be significant. But that hardly means you'll seize that opportunity. Significance defined as our culture would define it is simply a myth.

The reality is that possessions, power and position are all temporary in this life. They're nice while you have them. But, they typically do not last. Many have found themselves relying upon any or all of those things only to find themselves still drifting throughout life.

I believe you need three things to live a significant and intentional life. Three things that will eliminate accidental drift in your life. Here's how I would define true significance...

FACT:
Significance = MATURITY + MINISTRY + MISSION

In this definition, now you'll find yourself expressing God. Everything you live for will express God. How others think of you will be determined by how you express God. The legacy which you leave behind will express God. You see here's what I know about our world...

You'll either express God
or you'll eclipse God!

An eclipse is defined as an "event where an astronomical object is obscured."[1] Think of a total solar eclipse where the moon passes in front of the sun and prohibits you from seeing the sun. Unfortunately, in our lives that happens way too often. Whether we're talking about church, your home, your workplace - in every area of our lives - we find ourselves too often getting in God's way. The one who will make a true significant difference in this world will be the one who expresses God. Not the one who eclipses God.

---

1 "Eclipse," Wikipedia, section goes here, accessed February 13, 2015, http://en.wikipedia.org/wiki/Eclipse.

I believe as you begin to express God, you'll not only discover significance in your own personal life, but you'll also discover how to be significant in the lives of others.

My prayer for you is that you stop drifting randomly throughout your life. My prayer is that you begin to discover a significant purpose for your life and begin living intentionally for His cause. While there are many avenues to discovering that purpose, I can tell you the starting point. Just like if you are married, your marriage began with a relationship. The same is true as a follower of Christ. To discover why God created you, it begins by getting to know Him. The only way to know God is to hang out with God. Spend time with God. Get to know God on a personal level.

Following Christ isn't just a one-time decision. It's actually a daily one. It's a process. It's not that you have to get saved again each day. It's more of a reaffirmation. Luke records in his gospel when Jesus says...

> *If any of you wants to be my follower, you must turn from your selfish ways, take up your cross daily, and follow me.* (Luke 9:23)

We'll talk later about what it means to "take up your cross." That doesn't exactly mean the same thing in our culture today where we wear crosses around our neck, tattoo them on our chests and nail them to our kitchen walls. Knowing what it means to take up your cross daily will help you discover your purpose and significance in this life.

Here's the thing, though. God won't force you to pursue any kind of purpose and significance in your life. You have to make that choice and accept it for yourself. As a matter of fact, no one can make that choice but you. You can choose to follow His ways and His plans, or you can choose to follow your own way. Following your own way is what we would call sin. It's living outside of God's desires for your life. Sin will weave its way into every area of your life. From your family to your job, finances, etc. More often than not, sin results in a life of drifting.

Transforming Your Scale...

I know this may sound counter-intuitive, but there's nothing you can do to save yourself. I'll be honest, I used to believe I could save myself. If I were completely vulnerable, I'd have to admit that I still struggle to make up for my own wrongs. That's because, like you, I have a scale.

Have you ever noticed that we have scales for everything in our lives? All of humanity is based on scales. The education system is based on a grading scale. The speed limit is based on a speed scale. Sound is rated on the decibel scale. Length and height are nothing more than scales. Money is based on a scale. And, I hate to bring it up, but our weight is based on a scale as well. We base our entire lives on scales.

Even how we feel about ourselves is based on a scale. You'll wake up one morning and feel pretty good about life. Then the next morning you'll wake up and life looks bland. One day things go well for you on the job, but the next day they aren't as smooth. One day your marriage seems to be going along pretty well. Then the next day you start bickering about something petty (like what brand of toilet paper to buy) and your marriage feels like it's going down the tubes.

How you view life, how you view your job, how you view your marriage, how you view every situation in your life is completely based upon a scale. In every one of those situations, your scale is totally different from the next person. Scales are also how we judge ourselves and how holy or how human we feel. You see, everyone has a scale for measuring their holiness!

Everyone has a scale for measuring their holiness!

Are you familiar with your scale? I'm guessing you have one. Most people do. I do. I really wrestle with my scale. It's a daily struggle for me. My scale is hidden deep within my heart and my mind. If you look hard enough, I'm sure you would find yours. You can't get rid of your scale. However, your scale can be transformed. Rather than allowing Jesus to transform our scales, we opt to try and achieve balance via our own strength.

Let me explain. Imagine a scale similar to a teeter-totter. One side represents your humanness. The other side represents your holiness. (FYI: nonbelievers have the same scale, they'll just use different language to describe their two sides like good vs. bad, or moral vs. immoral.) Here's what you do. You sin. You mess up and now there's added weight on the humanness side of your scale. Then you say something that hurts someone. Toxic words spew from your mouth before you really think about the potency of what you're saying and you hurt somebody. More weight is added to the humanness side of your scale. You step back and observe your scale. You think to yourself, "I'm all out of balance!" You observe the scale tipping towards the humanness side and you react precisely as I would. You think to yourself that you have to make up for the wrong you've committed.

So, what do you do? You do something that you feel, in your own mind, will make up for the evil you just did. You help somebody out and weight is added to the holiness side of your scale. You take another look at your scale only to find that it's still tipping toward the humanness side. You have to do something else to make up for the wrong you've done. So, you don't just go to church on Sunday morning, you sing the songs with gusto. Maybe you put more money in the offering plate than normal. With each kind deed, in your mind, you think you've made up for the negative things you did earlier.

Again, you step back and observe your scale. Balance has been achieved because you've equaled your bad deeds with good deeds. The result is this. You feel pretty good about yourself. I don't know why, but we all have this internal scale that we use to measure the difference between our holiness and our humanness.

Have you ever had one of those internal arguments with yourself in your mind? I argue with myself all the time, and sometimes not silently. If so, then you have fought this scale in your life. If you have ever felt overwhelmed with guilt for something you did or something you said then you've fought the scale. The problem is that there's absolutely nothing you can do to achieve balance in your life between your humanness and your holiness. It's simply not within your grasp.

Here's the good news, though. Jesus looked upon you and saw your scale. He then took your scale and gave it a makeover. He took your scale, transformed it into a cross and then used it to make an eternal difference in your life. You see, the only way you can achieve balance in your life is to give your scale up to Jesus. When Jesus died on the cross, He died so that you would no longer have to be consumed with achieving balance. That scale you fight against day after day no longer has any effect on the outcome of your life. Balance comes through the cross.

Choose Your Tension...
So, the tension you live under in your life will be completely your choice. Tension isn't a bad thing in certain situations. I'll admit that tension in your marriage might not be desirable. Tension in

your workplace might be uncomfortable. Some tension is actually healthy. For example, I wear a belt almost every day. With the proper amount of tension, the belt functions properly. However, if there is not enough tension I risk my pants falling down (and trust me, no one wants to see that). On the other hand, if there is too much tension, I won't be able to breathe (probably more people than I'd like to admit would like to see that).

Do you own a car? If you do, then your car requires the proper amount of tension to get you from point A to point B. Pop the hood of your car and look down and you'll see a belt, or maybe two or three belts depending on your car. Those belts are critical to the performance of your car. They wind down and around all the intricate systems of your engine. Too little tension and the belt will slip preventing the car from moving. Too much tension and the belt will snap. Either way you look at it, the proper amount of tension is a good thing.

Tension is exactly the same in your day to day life. Without enough tension, you'll slip. With too much tension, you'll snap. The proper amount of tension, however, will propel you from point A to point B in your life. The choice is yours. You can continue to live under the tension of your scale and constantly try to achieve balance, or you can begin to live under the tension of the cross. The tension of the cross is where you will find complete freedom, significance and purpose for your life. You've already taken your first step towards defeating drift in your life. Now let's discover how to make defeating drift a daily routine!

CHAPTER 1

Defeating The Drift: Reading Your Bible

At the risk of losing my man card, I'm going to be vulnerable with you for just a moment. I don't go around talking about this to just anybody, but I can trust you, right? Here goes: I am a really big fan of Disney princesses.
There. I said it.

Say what you want, but I love Disney princesses. I don't know how you feel about them but – don't take this the wrong way – frankly, I don't care because I love Disney princesses.

My favorite Disney princess is Ariel. I guess it's the red hair. (Ok, so I know that sounds a little creepy, but just hear me out.) There are a lot of Disney princesses. Maybe you like Rapunzel best, the one with the mile-long hair that has magical healing powers. Or maybe your favorite is Tiana from *The Princess and the Frog*, or Belle from *Beauty and the Beast*. They're all wonderful characters and great role models. What's not to like?

But before you start jumping to conclusions about me, let me tell you why I know so much about Disney princesses, and more than that, why I even care.

I didn't grow up caring about princesses. Even throughout the early years of my marriage, you wouldn't have caught me watching

Snow White while cuddling with my wife. But then something happened on November 23, 2004 that changed my relationship with Disney princesses – and my life – forever.

On that day, God brought someone into my life who cares a lot about Disney princesses. And she means more to me than the sun, moon, and stars put together. If you have a daughter who loves princesses as much as my daughter does, then you probably love princesses too. I know this because you can't have a close relationship with someone and not care about what they care about!

> **You can't have a close relationship with someone and not care about what they care about!**

That fact applies to every area of your life. Maybe you don't have kids so you can't relate to that example. Let's try another one.

Let's say you're a guy dating a girl. She is smokin' hot, right!? She's smart. She's funny. She's everything you've always dreamed of. When you think of someone you want to spend the rest of your life with, she's the only one who comes to mind. But there's just one hang up: she's a vegetarian… a full-blown, animal rights, I-don't-wanna-eat-meat vegetarian. You, on the other hand, can't imagine life without a great side of medium-rare beef, maybe a couple of times a week. Besides her, there isn't anything that looks better to you than a nice, thick slab of rare Porterhouse coming off the grill and onto your plate.

For some guys, the prospect of a vegetarian girlfriend could be a deal breaker. But if you really believe she's the one for you, the one you want to spend your life with, then you just might find yourself trying to understand, or at least respect, her point of view.

That's because it's impossible to care about someone and not care about what they care about.

It's exactly the same when it comes to your relationship with Christ. You can't have a close relationship with Christ and not care about what He cares about. And in order to care about the things that Christ cares about, you'll have to do some digging rather than drifting.

Truth + Understanding = THEORY = PRACTICE...

Finish this sentence. Practice makes _____. If you're like most people, you probably said, "Perfect," right? After all, that's what we were taught and we believe to be true. Allow me to let you in on a little secret -- it's **absolutely false**. Surprised? I'll bet you are, but there is nothing factual in that statement. Practice does not make PERFECT; practice makes PERMANENT. If you practice something – anything – the wrong way over and over and over, you'll be instilling that wrong way into yourself as surely as if you intended it. You don't have to be a rocket scientist to know that if you practice something the wrong way, the outcome will always be anything less than perfect. That is simply reality. In other words, if you keep doing what you've always done, you'll keep getting what you've always got.

If you want to have a close relationship with Christ, the reality is that you must dig into and discover what Christ cares about. If you continue to practice what you think are the right ways, and those ways are not in sync with the ways of Christ, then you'll never get it right and you'll never grow. The Bible is packed full of wisdom about *truth and understanding*. For example...

> *In the beginning was the Word, and the Word was with God, and the Word was God.* (John 1:1)

Jesus answered, "I am the way and the truth and the life. No one comes to the Father except through me. If you really know me, you will know my Father as well. (John 14:6-7)

Read – Really READ – Your Bible...

As a pastor, I hesitate to say this, but too many followers of Christ are really just living out their parents' faith, or their grandparents' faith, or beliefs that a friend or a pastor has told them in the past. They may have gone to church all their lives, but have simply accepted the messages the preacher told them. They never actually rolled up their sleeves and put some elbow grease into understanding what it really means to have a meaningful relationship with Christ. No relationship can grow and flourish without time and attention. If you want to know Christ's truth, then there is no substitute for digging into your Bible and hanging out with Jesus. If you've never done this, then you may be living out someone else's beliefs rather than the principles the Bible actually teaches. And wouldn't you really rather find out for yourself? You see, if you don't dig into God's word, your beliefs may not be your own!

**If you don't DIG into God's Word,
your beliefs may not be your own!**

Now here's another bit of news. Just reading the Bible isn't enough. You have to read it. Then read it again. Then really dig into God's Word and allow it to penetrate you to your core. You have to think about it. You have to believe it. You have to feel it. You have to understand what it means in your life. The Psalmist writes...

Guide me in your truth and teach me, for you are God my Savior, and my hope is in you all day long. (Psalm 25:5)

Hungry and Confused...

A few years ago, I was leading a small group of 20-somethings. My wife and I have a passion for working with college-aged people and we were seeking to help them discover what their lives could look like centered in Christ.

One study focused on a booklet of suggested daily Bible readings that we would follow throughout the week. At the next meeting, a young lady spoke up and shared her frustrations about understanding her Bible. She was hungry for more. She was desperate for as much of God as she could possibly absorb. But she found herself discouraged because she couldn't understand a single word in her Bible. My first instinct was to ask her what translation of the Bible she was using, and I will never forget her reaction.

Her eyes got big and round and she expressed confusion. She asked me what I was talking about. She had no idea that there are a myriad of Bible translations available. It turned out she was reading the old-school King James Version – you know, the one filled with "thees" and "thous." After that meeting, some of us chipped in a few dollars and went Bible hunting for her.

I understood the difficulties the young lady was having. When I was growing up, we had an enormous Bible that sat centered on our coffee table year round. (You know what I'm talking about, right!? The kind you could use a weapon!) On Christmas morning, we always read the Christmas story about the birth of Jesus from that specific Bible. Let me tell you, that thing was intimidating even when it was closed. It was about two feet long and a foot thick. And if that were not enough, can you guess what translation it was? You got it -- the old school King James. I probably shouldn't admit this, but in spite of my good Christian upbringing and the efforts of my good Christian parents, I never got a thing out of that story on Christmas morning. For one, I didn't really understand a word of it. Plus, I might have been a little distracted by those presents under the tree!

Your Bible is the single most valuable tool in your life as a follower of Christ. Wait... Let me rephrase that. A Bible you can *understand* is the single most valuable tool in your life as a follower of Christ. Why? Because the Bible is God's word. It is a gift to you.

Even though the Bible has been translated many times throughout the years and into nearly every language in the world, it is still infallible. It is without error. Nelson Searcy writes, "The Bible is comprised of 66 books that were written over a period of 1500 years. The books were written by over 40 different authors from different places with different life experiences. These authors did not collaborate with one another. In many instances, they didn't even speak the same language."[2]

Non-believers may use those facts to claim that there's no possible way for the Bible to remain authentic and infallible. However, everything depends on your point of view. Where some might see a book tarnished by human hands over many centuries, I see a miracle performed by the very hands of God Himself. He has preserved and protected his word so that we might come to know Him personally. Most of us have never seen a miracle with our very own eyes, so it's hard to believe they even occurred. Miracles just aren't logical. After all, the Bible is just a book, right? In fact, in today's culture, the Bible seems to be viewed by many as a set of guidelines, or maybe a book of wisdom rather than the actual words of God, our Creator.

Think about this. Right before the 2012 Summer Olympics in London, I showed a video in Christ's Church about the history of the Olympic Games. That video said 2012 would mark the

---

2 Nelson Searcy, *The Next Step For Your Journey* (N.p.: n.p., 2012), 16.

third time London hosted the games, and that the first time was in 1908. Now, I happen to know for a fact (because I checked) that no one at Christ's Church was around in 1908. So not a single one of us could personally verify that the Olympics were held in London in that year. Yet, we don't doubt it. Why, then, do we doubt the records and stories we read in the Bible? Why do we feel the need to witness a miracle with our own eyes to know the truth of what has been reported?

Doubt VS. Faith...

Personally, I have no such doubts. A conversation with a colleague one day made me ask myself why. Why do some people automatically doubt while others – others like me – seem to just accept the Bible on what amounts to blind faith? For me, the answer is somewhere in my upbringing and coming of age. I grew up in a strong Christian family; I went to a strong Christian church that preached the Bible every week. The messages I heard were consistent no matter where I went. They were all messages of God's word in the Bible. In addition, I spent many years studying the word of God at the several Christian colleges I attended. But even with all of that, I don't have any more hard evidence than you do, or that a non-believer does, that would "prove" the Bible's veracity.

I was talking this over with my wife one day. She told me a story about when her mother was serving as a youth minister. Some of the kids in the youth group, she said, truly were believers. They believed in God and in God's word. But they didn't necessarily believe in the truth of some of the stories in the Bible. Some of it seemed just a bit far-fetched to them. I mean really, a guy gets swallowed up by a big fish and lives to tell about it? Yeah, right.

And herein lies one of the great Christian conundrums: If I believe only those parts of God's word that I choose to believe, am I a believer? If I have faith in only some of God's words, am I faithful?

Remember, if believing was easy, and provable, and evidence-based, it wouldn't be called faith! You see, your heart cannot rejoice in what your mind rejects!

—⚎—

**Your heart cannot rejoice
in what your mind rejects!**

—⚎—

In other words, if your mind is telling you that the stories you are reading in the Bible are just stories, then you will never *fully* connect with this God of the Bible. Even some 2,000 years after it was written, through the barriers and hurdles that might cause us to question, I still have full confidence that the Bible is without error and fully reliable. Have you read it lately? The writer of Hebrews says...

> *For the word of God is alive and active. Sharper than any double-edged sword, it penetrates even to dividing soul and spirit, joints and marrow; it judges the thoughts and attitudes of the heart.* (Heb. 4:12)

In other words, the Bible is not just a book. It's not just a collection of guidelines or a pile of paper bound in leather with your name inscribed on the front cover. It is God's inspired word which He used man to physically write. It is a life manual for you and me. William Barclay writes, "When people take God seriously, they immediately realize that his word is not only something to be studied, not only something to be read, not only something to be written about; it is something to be done."³ I believe inside you will discover purpose for your life.

Did you know the Bible is a best seller year after year? Did you know there are more than 500 translations? Did you know that the Bible has been translated into more than 2,200 languages? That's all good news, but at the same time, less than half of the adults in the United States strongly believe the Bible is totally accurate in its principles and teachings. So it leaves us with questions. Can I really trust this book? Can I truly believe what the Apostle Paul wrote to Timothy...

> All scripture is given by inspiration of God, and is profitable for doctrine, for reproof, for correction, for instruction in righteousness; that the man of God may be perfect, thoroughly furnished unto all good works. (2 Tim. 3:16-17)

If someone has weighed the options, looked at the Bible, and made a decision not to believe, nothing I can say – nothing even Paul can say – will convince them. But there is something I can do. I can continue to be unshakable in my faith and I can continue to pursue a life that follows the model of a good Christian that is presented in the Bible. And in doing that, I become the living proof, the evidence, of the truth of God's word. I could tell you all day long that I'm a trustworthy person. But it's only your experience with me over time that will prove to you I really am. I am God's evidence, and you are too. We are the evidence of the truth of this amazing book.

Biblical Uniqueness...

---

3 William Barclay, *The Letter To The Hebrews* (Louisville, KY: Westminster John Knox Press, 1976), 47.

There is no other book in the world like the Bible – it is unique in so many ways.

The Bible is unique in its continuity. Even though the Bible was written by 40 successive generations over 1,500 years and its authors varied from paupers to kings who lived on three different continents, its message is consistent from beginning to end.

The Bible is unique in its circulation. Thirty years ago, Hy Pickering said that to keep up with demand, the British and Foreign Bible Society had to turn out a copy of the Bible every three seconds.[4] Even if that figure is lower now, we'd have to add to it the number of times the Bible is downloaded in digital form, which wasn't available 30 years ago.

The Bible is unique in its translation. In the 1950s and 1960s, there were more than 3,000 translators working on translations of the Bible. I wonder why they bothered if it's just another book?

The Bible is unique in its survival. Even though it was written on material that would perish over time, the Bible has survived. In fact, as compared to other ancient texts, the Bible has more manuscript evidence than any ten other pieces of classical literature combined.

The Bible is unique in its teachings. There is no better example of this than in the prophecies of the Bible. Over and over again, the Bible has always proven itself. Check out what Peter writes...

> *Above all, you must understand that no prophecy of Scripture came about by the prophet's own interpretation of things. For prophecy never had its origin in the human will, but prophets, though human, spoke from God as they were carried along by the Holy Spirit.* (1 Pet. 1:20-21)

---

4 "Evidence That Demands a Verdict - Ch. 1 - The Uniqueness of the Bible," Evidence That Demands a Verdict - Ch. 1 - The Uniqueness of the Bible, section goes here, accessed February 16, 2015, http://www.angelfire.com/sc3/myredeemer/Evidencep3.html.

So when the Bible predicts the coming of the Messiah, that prophecy is coming directly from God and not from the human mind attached to the hands that wrote it down.

It comes down to this: Deny the authority of the Bible, and you deny the authority of God. D.L. Moody once said, "The scriptures were not given for our information but our transformation."[5]

Choosing A Bible Translation...

There is a wide range of translations available to you today. In our modern, digital age, one of the greatest tools for you is the *YouVersion* app.[6] It's free to download and contains virtually every Bible translation you could ever desire. I encourage you to download it and try out several translations before investing in the real book. Some common, easy to read English translations are the *New International Version*, the *New Living Translation*, and the *English Standard Version*. There are also "paraphrase" Bibles such as *The Message*. It's written in story format; however, it isn't a true translation, as paraphrase implies. But if you come across a verse that is difficult to understand, flipping over to *The Message* may help.

Where Do I Start...

I've been reading the Bible my whole life and I'll admit, it can still sometimes be overwhelming. Sixty-six books. Old Testament and New Testament. History books. Books of poetry and books of the prophets. The Gospel accounts. The list goes on.

I want to make sure you start in the right place, as there are places that are very difficult to understand. If you happened to

---

5 "A Quote by D.L. Moody," Goodreads, section goes here, accessed February 16, 2015, http://www.goodreads.com/quotes/239061-the-bible-was-not-given-for-our-information-but-for.

6 https://www.youversion.com

start in one of the tougher spots, your journey through the Bible might end before it begins.

A great place to start is with the book of James. It's only five chapters long and pretty clear-cut. James was the brother of Jesus, so to me, that lends some credibility to his words. Think about it. What would it take for your brother to convince you that he's the son of God? He's blunt and to the point – a real straightforward guy.

Here's what I want you to do. Don't try to read the entire book at one time. Even if you're one of those pathetically fast readers (and by the way, if that's you, you make me sick). Be disciplined and read just one section at a time. You'll see the sections. Most Bibles are already split up with titles for each section. Next, get a journal, open up a document on your computer, or get a journal app on your notepad. Note the date and which passage you read. Then write two or three sentences about something that stood out to you in what you just read. Is there a promise that is made? Maybe there's a warning or a command to follow. Maybe the passage is pointing out a sin with which you may be struggling. Whatever it is, write it down. This will literally take you no more than five minutes a day. The key is consistency, day after day. It's a habit you need to build into your life.

Now, go back to the beginning. Really look at the Bible passage you just read. Has it clicked yet? Remember, the Bible is God's inspired words, so you're not just reading a book. Rather, God is speaking to you, and the words you just wrote down reflects the message he wants you to know and learn in that very moment. How cool is that? To know that the Creator of this giant universe wants to speak to you! That's called... Defeating the DRIFT!

No Cherry Picking...

Ever picked cherries off of a tree? Unless you've developed a technique I don't know about, there's only one way to do it – one at a time. So how does that compare to reading the Bible? As you read, you may find yourself drawn to one passage or another, things that might hold special meaning for you. It may be tempting to focus just on those passages. If you were, you wouldn't be the first. That's one of the dangers when it comes to reading the Bible. People, being people, tend sometimes to seek out things that agree with what they already believe, know, or think they know. When they do, there is great potential to exclude the rest of the message. They may take things out of context to reinforce their own beliefs, offering them as "proof" to others.

Here's a classic example: Preachers love to get on their soapbox and pound Romans 3:23 down the throats of those listening. That passage says...

> ...for all have sinned and fall short of the glory of God, (Rom. 3:23)

Did you notice that the first word is not capitalized? It's obviously not the first word of the sentence. Even the word "for" in this context is a connecting word. It's connecting something before it to something after it. Also, did you notice the comma at the end? There must be more. But some preachers will take those twelve words and slam their fists down proclaiming the evilness in us all. Have you ever experienced that? I have. I walk away feeling like the worst person on planet earth.

Now, before I continue, let me quickly agree with the facts in that brief sentence. The fact is that we all have sinned. The fact is that we have all fallen short of God's glory. However, I'm afraid that the verse alone is an incomplete truth. There is more that God wants you to know. There's more to the equation. Check out the full passage in its context...

> *This righteousness is given through faith in Jesus Christ to all who believe. There is no difference between Jew and Gentile,*

> *for all have sinned and fall short of the glory of God, and all are justified freely by his grace through the redemption that came by Christ Jesus.* (Rom. 3:22-24)

Suddenly that cherry-picked verse sandwiched right in the middle takes on a completely new tone. Either way, that cherry-picked verse is still true. However, the point is that, even though we've all screwed up, God is still willing to set you free by the grace of Jesus Christ. I'd much rather hear that message than the out-of-context version. Wouldn't you?

So, when you're reading your Bible, always read the larger context. If you don't, you might move in the wrong direction. And that's what I mean by digging into your Bible.

The Lost Art of Meditation...
One of my favorite foods is teriyaki anything. Chicken, steak, shrimp, you name it. Here's the thing about teriyaki anything, though. If you toss a porterhouse side of beef on your grill and then baste it with teriyaki sauce, it will probably be okay. But the key to a really great teriyaki steak is giving it time to marinate. The natural flavors of that steak begin to transform into teriyaki flavors. I can hear it sizzling now! (Am I making you hungry yet?)

The thing about marinating, though, is it takes time. Sometimes I feel like we all need to slow down a little. We live in a world of freeways, corporate ladders, Playstations, and Xboxes. Everything happens fast, and there's never a break. We work hard. We play hard. Sometimes it seems like the hands on the clock move as fast as the blades on a rotary fan. It can get to you after a while. You feel beaten up and torn down. The burdens on your back feel as heavy as the world. Reading the Bible can provide you the opportunity to escape for a few minutes. Rest. Be still. Rejoice in your blessings. Hear God's word. Listen to His voice.

In this world where stillness and meditation are very difficult to achieve, our lives will be dominated by our outer world unless we make the time, to cultivate our inner world through reading the Bible and marinating on it. To me, meditation is just like marinating. Instead of just splashing some of God's word on yourself at the last minute, like maybe only in church on Sunday morning, try marinating on God's word. Meditate on it. Think about it day and night. Check out these passages...

> *Keep this Book of the Law always on your lips; meditate on it day and night, so that you may be careful to do everything written in it. Then you will be prosperous and successful.* (Josh. 1:8)
>
> *Oh, how I love your instructions! I think about them all day long.* (Ps. 119:97)
>
> *And Isaac went out to meditate in the field in the evening.* (Gen. 24:63)
>
> *I stay awake through the night, thinking about your promise.* (Ps. 119:148)
>
> *I lie awake thinking of you, meditating on you through the night.* (Ps. 63:6)

Give this a try. Take the book of James, or maybe First Peter, and read the entire book, once a day for a week. For James, you'd read all five chapters every day for seven days in a row. This will take you a little longer than five minutes like I mentioned earlier. If you're a pathetically slow reader like me, it might take you 20 to 30 minutes.

But, here's what will happen. Progressively each day, you'll begin to notice more and more. Even though you're reading the same words, different aspects will begin to jump out at you. You'll begin to ponder words and phrases that you wouldn't have given a second thought about with just one reading. God and His Holy Spirit will begin to transform you through this theological principle I call... marinating!

So, go ahead. Go get you a juicy rib-eye from the grocery store. (Maybe wrap some bacon around it because everyone knows bacon makes everything better!) Toss some teriyaki sauce on it. Get comfy, prop up your feet, and read James. When you're finished, grill that steak till it's a mouth-watering medium-rare thing of beauty. And dig into the Bible. Dig and dig and dig and allow God to use his word to penetrate you at your core.

The concept of meditation is throughout the entire Bible. Think back to the scripture passages in the previous section. Let me just repeat one of them...

> *I lie awake thinking of you, meditating on you through the night.* (Ps. 63:6)

I wanted to bring this up again because I love how *The Message* paraphrases that verse. Remember what I mentioned in the previous chapter about different Bible translations and paraphrases? This is a great example. *The Message* paraphrases that verse like this...

> *I eat my fill of prime rib and gravy; I smack my lips. It's time to shout praises! If I'm sleepless at midnight, I spend the hours in grateful reflection. Because you've always stood up for me, I'm free to run and play. I hold on to you for dear life, and you hold me steady as a post.* (The Message, Ps. 63:6)

Ok, so maybe I like the reference to prime rib. Have you gotten the impression yet that I wouldn't make a very good vegetarian?

With that passage in mind, exactly what is the goal of meditating on God's word? Simply said, the goal is having the ability to hear God's voice and obey His word.

The goal is the ability to hear God's voice and obey His word.

There are no hidden mysteries.

There's no secret sauce.

Seems simple, right? The fact is this: God, the Creator of the universe, desires to have a relationship with you.

In the Garden of Eden, Adam and Eve talked with God and God talked with them. Then came the fall. They were cast out of the garden. And ever since, man has been running away – and God has been chasing us. In story after story in the Bible, we see God reaching out. There was Cain, Abel, Noah, Abraham – God was speaking and teaching and guiding. It is through meditation that we develop the ability to hear God's voice and obey His word.

Let me share four basic steps to reading your Bible and meditating upon it:

1. Repetition

My wife and I love watching the Olympics. There might not be a better example anywhere of people who have developed such great disciplines. Not only do they train for hours upon hours every day, they also study videos of themselves training. They study their opponents' every move. They study the physical and environmental conditions associated with their sport. And they work just as hard at that as they do on training their bodies. What would motivate a person to put forth that kind of effort? They know it's the only way they can transform themselves into the kind of athletes they want to be. And what brings them back day after day? They know that repetition forms habits. Richard Foster stated, "We must realize that sheer repetition without understanding what is being repeated affects the inner mind. Ingrained habits of thought can be formed by repetition alone, thus changing behavior."[7] Such is the force of repetition alone, but there's more to reading your Bible and meditation.

2. Concentration

I've talked a little about focus and here is where it really comes into play. To get as much as possible out of reading your Bible, it takes slowing down and concentrating on what you are reading. Recently, I realized something about my own work habits. Typically, I come into my office in the morning, start up my computer, and check my email. Then I spend a little time responding to and sending emails before moving on to other things. Typically I leave my email open all day. So no matter what I was doing and no matter how much concentration it required, I would be frequently interrupted by my computer telling me I had a new email. Not only that, my curiosity would drive me crazy if I didn't check to see who emailed me. So I would stop whatever I was doing to check (after all, I'm an important person and people need constant access to me).

---

7 Richard J. Foster, *Celebration Of Discipline: The Path To Spiritual Growth* (San Francisco, CA: Harper San Francisco, 1978), 64-65.

Here's what I had learned. First, I learned that I'm not all that important after all. Second, I learned that others actually do not need instant access to me. I also learned that through daily repetition, I had formed a not-so-productive habit of allowing my concentration to waiver and be broken... simply by leaving my email open. So now after I finish with my email in the morning, I shut it down while I am doing other things. Then I open it up again at intervals throughout the day when it's appropriate.

What is it that you need to do to enable a higher level of concentration? Maybe set your cell phone to the side. Or, better yet, turn it completely off for a while. I promise you, the world will keep on spinning. Remember that passage earlier where Jesus got away to a "lonely" place? That's impossible to do if the technology that surrounds you enables others access to you.

3. Comprehension

John 8:32 tells us that the truth will set us free. By concentrating on God's word it will lead to a greater comprehension for His will in your life. It's comprehension that will help you understand His truth and figure out how to apply it in your life.

If you're like me, sometimes you may have to read something two or three times before it begins to really sink in. One thing that helps is to pause after each section and ask yourself what the text is really saying. If you just think about it for a minute, you'll know whether you've comprehended what you read. If not, read it again. Next, ask yourself what the text really means in context. By that I mean it's easy for us to look at something in isolation and assign meaning to it that actually has nothing to do with the author's intentions. That's called *cherry-picking* like I mentioned earlier. Ask questions such as: Why did the author write this passage? To whom did he write it? When did he write it? What was the everyday culture like when he wrote it? The answers to those questions will often reveal a much greater comprehension to what God is trying to communicate with you. If you don't know the answers to those questions, a quick Google search will give you ample information.

4. Reflection

The final step in reading your Bible is reflection. It's through reflection that we can assign the appropriate level of significance to what we are reading. This is the step where you figure out how what you're reading applies to your own life. Because through reflection we not only come to understand our subject matter, but ourselves as well!

> **Through reflection we not only come to understand our subject matter, but ourselves as well!**

Jesus often speaks of ears that do not hear and eyes that do not see. Reflection on what you are studying opens you to hearing and seeing in a whole new way. Practicing these four steps will help you to develop a strong discipline allowing God to speak to you through His word.

CHAPTER 2

Defeating The Drift: Un-Learning To Pray

> *"The prayer of a righteous man is powerful and effective,"* James 5:16

'm sure this will sound extremely elementary, but the best description of prayer I can think of is this... I talk and He listens! He talks and I listen!

—⁂—

I talk and He listens! He talks and I listen!

—⁂—

Elementary, right!?
I believe it really is as simple as that, though.
I have spoken with so many folks over the years who have taken their prayer life to a whole new level of difficulty. For me, one of the first things I think of is growing up sitting around the dinner table, hands held together, eyes closed and heads bowed. Did you grow up like that? Or, maybe it was your nightly prayers

on your knees at the side of your bed. If you grew up attending church every Sunday like I did, then I'm guessing you might have thought about the pastor's prayer where he speaks while the rest of us sit there in silence.

I want you to know that prayer is not a difficult thing. It's as simple as talking to God just like He's a real person sitting next to you.

See, for many people, their presumptions of how prayer should look, sound, and feel make prayer difficult for them. We've been groomed throughout our entire lives to say all the right things and do all the right things in prayer. If you don't, then you're not good at praying.

Do you ever feel like that?
You don't know what to say.
Dear God... I don't know what else to say.
Do you bow your heads and close your eyes?
What if I can't pray like other people?

If there were stipulations and qualifications that validate your prayers then the Apostle Paul would have never instructed us to "pray without ceasing."[8] Obviously if you are required to close your eyes and bow your head in order to pray then you can't be driving down the highway while praying (at least I wouldn't advise it). Prayer is so much simpler than what we typically make it out to be! For that reason I want to give you some practical tips here for staying in touch with God through prayer.

It's All About Communication...

Are you married? Even if you're not, I bet you still know that if you're going to develop a lasting relationship with someone that it requires a little communication. Do you know what would happen if I ceased talking with my wife? Trust me, it would not be a good

---
8 English Standard Version, 1 Thes. 5:17

thing. Everything would fall apart. It wouldn't be long before we would find ourselves heading in two totally different directions in life. The only way for me to know her deepest desires in life is to talk with her.

Do you know what gets in the way of healthy communication with my wife?

Busyness!

I'm a busy man and I'll be honest with you. The more busy I am, the more important I feel. The more others need me, the more valued I feel. I don't mind the busyness. I actually welcome it. But, the more busy I get, the less attention I give my wife. No, this isn't a book on how to improve your marriage, but I promise you, if you're married, you can apply that.

The same is true of your journey with God. Busyness isn't a bad thing, until it begins to alter your priorities. It's been said for years that Satan doesn't necessarily need to make us bad. He just has to keep us busy. And that busyness will deter you from all that is truly important in this life.

Add children into the mix and your life just got dramatically more busy. As they grow up, the daily demands seem to get more and more extreme. With sports, dance class, and recitals, the list goes on and on. Our intentions are noble. We want the best for our family, but I'm afraid our quest for good will deter our quest for the best.

There is just one simple requirement to solid, healthy communication. Intentionality. In fact, nothing in this book will help you apart from intentional actions! It took me years to discover the benefit of sitting down with my wife every payday to discuss our financial situation. Now I can't remember the last time we had an argument about money. I'm not saying that we have more money, but simple and intentional communication has drastically improved our financial condition.

Your intentional time in prayer will improve your condition!

Your intentional time in prayer will open your heart towards others.

Your intentional time in prayer will soften your outlook in tense situations.

Why? Because you are what you pray!

You Are What You PRAY!!!

You know that phrase... "You are what you eat"? Like, I'm going to turn into a Twinkie because I eat them by the box (and I do). Or, my daughter is gonna turn into a chicken nugget (because there's nothing else she'll eat). I believe there's a lot of truth to that phrase when it comes to prayer.

I often compare life to surfing. Many of us set out in life grabbing the surf board and taking a lot of risk. The waves we ride are kinda small at first. Wave after wave comes and you feel pretty good about things. But then you look back and you see a big one coming. In that moment, what's your response? Many folks, rather than looking at that wave as a challenge see the possible failure.

Is that you?

You think about how you could fall, how you may crash. There are giant sharks in those waters below you and they're hungry. I bet you'd taste good too! So rather than standing and riding the wave, you get down on your knees. You play it safe because you don't want to get too radical.

Then you turn around and you see even a larger wave coming at you. It's fast. It's furious. This wave has failure written all over it. You don't stand. You're not down on your knees. I mean, let's be smart here! You opt for the safest place... lying completely down on your belly holding on for dear life. Do you know what happens when you lie down on the surf board and hold on? The wave passes you by!

Have you ever let the wave pass you by?

I have.

I regretted it too!

You've heard the phrase, "You're gonna miss the boat"? Well, in this case, you missed the wave. Surfers travel all over the globe in search of the perfect wave. I promise you when they find it, they won't miss it.

But, there's an even greater risk than missing the wave. For many folks in life, once they experience how comforting it is to just lie down and float on their bellies, they never get back up. Let's be honest. It doesn't take nearly as much energy lying down on the surf board than it does standing up trying to ride the wave.

It's relaxing.

I need to soak up some sun anyway.

Why not just lie here for a while and enjoy the simple life!?

This is exactly the path that many of us follow when it comes to prayer in our lives. We start out praying big prayers. Bold prayers. But shortly after, we begin to feel like maybe God isn't listening to our prayers.

Ever wondered if God hears your prayers?

I have!

I still do on a regular basis!

James 5:16 says that the "prayer of a righteous man is powerful and effective." But I hardly feel righteous. Does God really hear our prayers? It's a fair question. After all, God has to manage this entire universe, how can he have the time to hear my prayers!? And so our prayers get smaller and smaller... Less and less frequent... to the point where we find ourselves just floating through life.

Then I became a father. Do you have children? If so, then this will make sense. I love my daughter with everything within me. I would give my life for her. To say that God has blessed me with an angel would be an understatement (and when she brings a boy home for the first time, I will be on the front porch with a shotgun in one hand and my Bible in the other.)

It wasn't until I had a child that I began to understand God's love for me. In a room full of crazy kids, I can hear my daughter's voice over all the others. Do you know why? It's because I know her voice personally. Even as her voice has changed tone as she's grown up, I still know her voice. And, when my daughter speaks, her father listens.

When you speak, your Father listens too!

The next time you doubt whether God hears your prayers, remember that he knows your voice. In fact, he loves you so much that he died for you. That's what daddies do when they love their children.

Mark Batterson writes, "Prayers are prophecies. They are the best predictors of your spiritual future. Who you become is determined by how you pray. Ultimately, the transcript of your prayers becomes the script of your life."[9] In other words, you are what you pray! As a result of prayer, we not only accomplish great things through God, but God accomplishes great things through us!

Pick Up the Hotline...

I grew up listening to some stellar Christian rock music in the 80s. Ya know, the generation of *hair!*? One of my favorite bands was White Heart. They had an album titled "Hotline." The lyrics in the title track say, "Pick up the hotline, let Him know what's on your mind." I think, rather than viewing prayer as a phone line that we can always pick up and dial God's number, we need to start thinking of it more like the internet. (Granted, they didn't have internet when that song was written.) Prayer should be a constant connection, always on, always communicating (and I'm not talking dial-up. I'm talking high-speed fiber optics). The Apostle Paul writes...

---

9 Mark Batterson, The Circle Maker: Praying Circles around Your Biggest Dreams and Greatest Fears (Grand Rapids, MI: Zondervan, 2011), Loc 94 of 3690.

Rejoice always; pray without ceasing; in everything give thanks; for this is God's will for you in Christ Jesus. (1 Thes. 5:16-18)

Do you doubt your skills? Are you always comparing yourself to spiritual "giants" who use flashy, eloquent language when they pray? Ever been in one of those prayer circles where the leader instructs that you're going to pray around the circle, but if you don't want to pray just squeeze the next person's hand? In a circle of fifteen people, only two pray, the first person and then the last.

It happens all the time. It doesn't matter how young or old you are, there's just something about people and prayer. I've spoken with so many people who are scared to pray in public. I wonder how many people are scared to pray in private as well.

If you don't know what to say, Paul gives us some good advice in that passage. He tells us to "rejoice always." Do you know that part of your prayer can be rejoicing? It's easy to rejoice when your favorite football team scores the winning touchdown. Why can't you rejoice for what God has done for you? Paul also says to "give thanks." It's easy to be thankful in November during the Thanksgiving season. (Especially when a turkey and a pitcher of gravy are sitting on the table!) But, can you be thankful in the hurtful times?

When Paul tells us that "this is God's will for you," what's he talking about? Could it be that God loves you so much that he desires always to be with you? To always be with you would require that you are always with him! Prayer should be at the heartbeat of all you do because you are what you pray. What you pray will become the script of your life.

Why not take a minute now, grab a piece of paper and write down everything for which you are thankful. Next, take a few moments and thank God.

But I'm Not Good Enough To Pray!
Let me ask you a question.

Have you ever doubted God?

I've doubted God many times.

If we're honest with ourselves, every single follower of Christ has doubted God at one point or another. Most still do at times. We've all had those moments where we're surfing along. Life is good. We're riding wave after wave. Then all of a sudden a shark comes up and bites your leg off! (My best friend says that's why you shouldn't swim in the ocean!) I'll be vulnerable. I feel like such a hypocrite sometimes because I get up on stage almost every Sunday and preach about how big God is, how powerful God is, how God can take care of any problem you may have. Then the mail comes on Monday and there's an unexpected bill and in less than 5 seconds, I go from how God has everything under control to... "God, are you there!? Do you still love me?" We've all gone through times like that. It's in those moments that many folks begin to pray less and less because we doubt God. We feel unworthy. You'll tell yourself that you're simply not good enough to pray. But the fact is this, God loves the prayers of imperfect people!

God loves the prayers of imperfect people!

And it's a good thing because you're not perfect.

Neither am I.

Nobody is.

I believe one of the most important qualities of effective communication with God is gut-level honesty. Like I mentioned earlier, if I can't pray with flowery language like someone else, then I don't feel qualified to pray. It's just the way our human minds work. We always compare ourselves to others, but the fact is this; God doesn't have any favorites. He doesn't love your pastor more than you. He doesn't favor one child over another. In fact, unlike your grandma, he doesn't have to run through all the names of his children before he gets your name right! (I'm starting to do that already at my age... and I only have one child!) God just wants you to talk with him just like you would talk with your best friend.

Is he your best friend?

Maybe that's the problem!

At the peak of his ministry, Jesus preached his best sermon ever. This was the mac-daddy. It was his pinnacle teaching. His masterpiece, if you will. We call it the *Sermon On The Mount*. At one point Jesus says...

> *And when you pray, do not be like the hypocrites, for they love to pray standing in the synagogues and on the street corners to be seen by others.* (Matt. 6:5)

Take a stroll through the Gospels in the Bible and you'll find that Jesus never criticized prayers that were honest, only those that were showy. So don't pressure yourself to pray longer prayers filled with extravagant language like the spiritual "giants" you may look up to. Rather, shoot for more frequent prayer.

That's what Paul was talking about when he instructed us to "pray without ceasing." As you pray more frequently, your life will be more infused with a God-consciousness.

Do you know what a God-consciousness is?

When prayer is the heartbeat of all you do... you should find that you are developing a more frequent prayer life, like you're firing off rapid-fire prayers all day long. Have you heard of rapid-fire prayers?

Let me ask you this. If you're being attacked by zombies, would you rather have a rotary-gatling gun that can fire 2,000 rounds per minute, or a pistol that has to be reloaded every 6 rounds? A gun that fires 2,000 rounds per minute is called rapid-fire. Rather than praying a morning prayer, a prayer before your meals, and then a prayer at night, why not fire off one-liner prayers all day long? As you see the sunrise, thank God for the beauty. (And you ask God to give you a job that allows you to sleep in too!) When someone says something nice to you at your workplace, thank God for that person and ask God to bless him. Even when you butt heads with your spouse (hopefully not literally), you pray to God for more patience. See the difference? The result is you'll begin to see and hear God throughout your entire life, day after day, and you'll begin to develop a God-consciousness. God's heart will be more infused in your heart.

It means when you wake up in the morning you'll recognize God. When you go to bed at night, you'll know that God has been with you throughout the day. When you're at work and something goes haywire, you'll see God in your own outlook. Through the good, the bad, the positive and the negative, you'll know that God is surrounding you.

There's this guy in the Old Testament named Enoch. (Not the best name to give a boy in my opinion! Just saying.) We don't know much about him. We don't read a long life-story in the Bible about him like Moses or Abraham or David, but the Bible does provide us with some priceless information about Enoch. Check this out...

> Enoch walked faithfully with God; then he was no more, because God took him away. (Gen. 5:24)

At the end of the day, at the end of my life, if walking faithfully with God is all that people have to say about me, then I'm perfectly fine with that.

Unfortunately, most people miss that relationship with God. Instead, they depend on people rather than Christ for their spiritual experience. If you only attend your worship service on Sunday morning, you'll never fully experience an ongoing relationship with Christ. Even if you get plugged into a small group, or an accountability group. If you're not cultivating your relationship with God on your own, your experience with Him will be limited to your experiences with other people. Jesus goes on to say this in the *Sermon On The Mount...*

> *But seek first his kingdom and his righteousness, and all these things will be given to you as well.* (Matt. 6:33)

To seek God and His kingdom requires you to pray. There are all kinds of expressions throughout the Bible to show one's devotion to God, but there was none closer and none more intimate than to be described as one who walked with God, and you must talk with God to walk with God!

You must talk with God to walk with God!

Think about this in your physical sense. You can walk in front of someone. You can walk behind someone. But these are totally different from walking *with* someone. When you walk in front or behind someone there are times when you can do your own thing. However, when you walk *with* someone, that person knows everything about you. That person sees everything you do. In the long run, no doubt you will begin to share your dreams, your desires, your wishes with that person. That person knows your goals and how you'd like to impact this world. What if, rather than walking in front of God, or behind God, you began to walk *with* God? I love to hear my daughter talk about her dreams and what she wants to grow up to become one day. What if you began to share your dreams with God, your goals with God, your ideas with God? What if you began making jokes with God?

Whoa, whoa, whoa!

Joke with God!?

That doesn't sound like the God I learned about in church!

God created everything, right? Do you love to laugh? Do you love a good comedy at the movies? Do you love joking around with your friends? Well, the fact is that God made you that way. I'm guessing that if God created you to have fun, then God also loves to have fun. (Although, I'm fairly certain that God hates Laffy-Taffy jokes!) Here's the question. What if you began to reveal your entire life to Him?

I see so many folks get hung up on their laundry list of prayer requests. Do you know what I'm talking about? We have a list, our list of requests, and there's everything from someone who's sick to the next-door neighbor's cat. (Which would be better off dead because… well… it's a cat!) Don't hear me wrong. There's absolutely nothing wrong with the laundry list of prayer requests. God wants you to bring your requests to him. My point is simply this. There is so much more to prayer than treating God like your own personal genie where you expect to rub his lamp, make your wish, and presto.

Often times we treat God like a soda machine. If I put my money in, if I make my deposit, then God is supposed give me something in exchange. Therefore, our prayers just end up being a laundry list; a request list to God. God longs for so much more. You deserve so much more! However, as you begin to fire off rapid-fire prayers throughout the day, your focus is going to shift. That's because prayer shifts our focus from ourselves onto God!

Prayer Shifts Our Focus From Ourselves Onto God!

Maybe that's one reason more people don't pray.

They're too busy focussed on themselves to think about God.

Think about what your main goal in prayer is? What's the purpose of prayer? If your prayer life is dry and if you find that your prayers consist primarily of petitions and needs, then most likely your main goal in prayer is to control your environment rather than to delve into an intimate relationship with God who loves you. You see, prayer reminds you that you're not in control and keeps you close to the One who is. As you pray more, you're going to find that your opinions, your likes, your beliefs and your perspectives are going to begin to align with God's. That's because you are what you pray. Any genuine communication with God may or may not change what God does, but your prayer will often change your heart and perspective. Leonard Ravenhill writes, "A sinning man will stop praying, and a praying man will stop sinning."[10] Look at James one more time...

> *The prayer of a righteous person is powerful and effective.* (Jam. 5:16)

In other words, the effectiveness of your prayers will often be tied to the holiness of your life. Think about that. That's a little scary.

---

10 Leonard Ravenhill, Why Revival Tarries (Minneapolis: Bethany Fellowship, 1959), pg. #27.

The effectiveness of your prayers is often tied to the holiness of your life.

We can get into all kinds of theological debates about that statement. God's word is clear that He loves us all. He loves you just as much as he loves me. He loves you just as much as he loves one whom you might describe as a sinner... a murderer... or a rapist. God loves us all just as much as the next. But check this out...

The eyes of the LORD are on the righteous, and his ears are

attentive to their cry. (Ps. 34:15)

With that in mind, maybe our prayers should not begin with, here's my laundry list and now I expect you to take care of these things for me, God. Rather, maybe our prayers should begin... please forgive me.

Wash me clean.
I am a sinner.
Unworthy.

You are what you pray. Prayer is not a matter of bowing your head and closing your eyes. It's not required that you get down on your knees (while I would agree it is a humble position). To "pray without ceasing" means that you walk and talk with the Lord just the same as you do with your best friend. Don't worry about making your prayer sound formal. Don't worry about filling your prayer with flowery language. Just talk with Him.

Prayer Was Never Meant To Be A Monologue!

That's right. Prayer was never meant to be a one-way conversation where you do all the talking and God does all the listening. Prayer was meant to be a dialogue between you and God. The problem is that God doesn't exactly speak to us like your best friend talks to you (and if He has, I'd love to get to know you more!). So, if God doesn't talk to us verbally like everyone else, how are we supposed to hear God when He speaks?

It's really quite simple. The answer is in the previous chapter where we talked about reading your Bible. That's how God will speak to you.

Here's how you enter into a dialogue with God, you PRAY THROUGH THE BIBLE. Effective prayer begins by praying through the Bible. If the dialogue between you and God was scripted out for you, then prayer would be your part and God's response would be found in the Bible. You can also flip that around as well. Scripture is God's way of initiating conversations and prayer is our response. This mindset shift happens when we begin to realize that the Bible was never meant to be simply read through. Most people in our day and age see the Bible as just another book. Even though we call it "God's Word," we still treat it just like another book to read. But the Bible was meant to be prayed through. And if you pray through it, I promise you that you'll never run out of things to talk about with God.

Reading is the way you get *through* the Bible...

Prayer is the way you get the Bible through *you!*

That's why I define prayer as you talking and God listening, and then God talking and you listening.

Amen!

CHAPTER 3

Defeating The Drift: Connecting With Church

You've screwed up before, haven't you? Even if I've never met you, here's what I know about you. It doesn't matter what you believe about Christianity, whether you are a sold-out follower of Christ, or even if you question whether Jesus was truly the Son of God. I know that you've made at least one mistake in your life. Most likely you've made many. I also know this - you'll make another mistake before you die.

But here's the thing. In our humanity, we often define ourselves by those mistakes. Just take a look at the news and most likely you'll hear at least one story about a famous person who made a mistake. Hopefully you've never heard your surgeon say "Oops!" Hopefully, the pilot of your plane doesn't still have any mistakes up his sleeve. BUT, how many times have you gone to the beach and forgotten to put on sunscreen? We've all made mistakes.

There is a classic story that Luke records for us in chapter fifteen of his gospel. If you've been a part of the church for any length of time, no doubt you've heard the story. It's the story of The Prodigal Son.

Basically, there is a man who has two sons. The younger son goes to his father and says he wants his share of the estate NOW instead of waiting and his father agrees. So the boy packs up all his stuff and he splits. He takes off. He goes to a distant land, wastes all of his money, and one day wakes up broke. A famine hits, so now he's hungry. He gets a job feeding pigs. He's so hungry that he's willing to eat the same scraps that he's feeding the pigs (My grandparents used to be farmers and I've see what those scraps look like. YUK!) But then we're told that he comes to his senses. Check this out...

> "When he came to his senses, he said, 'How many of my father's hired servants have food to spare, and here I am starving to death! I will set out and go back to my father and say to him: Father, I have sinned against heaven and against you. I am no longer worthy to be called your son; make me like one of your hired servants.' (Luke 15:17-19)

Did you catch that last part? The son considers himself unworthy to be called his father's son any longer. He allowed his mistakes to define him as a person. What I want you to know is that your destiny is not determined by your mistakes but by your identity!

—ɯ—

Your destiny is not determined by your mistakes but by your identity!

—ɯ—

I have made a lot of mistakes throughout my life. I've screwed up as a husband. I've messed up as a father. I've made dumb decisions financially. I've jacked up my career. You name it, I've probably made a mistake in that area of my life. But, here's what my Dad taught me a long, long time ago. While I need to learn from those mistakes, those mistakes will never change the fact that I am his son.

I wonder if you need to hear that today.

Do you know that you know that you know that there is nothing that can change the fact that you are your Father's son or daughter! And instead of continuing to run AWAY from home, you need to run BACK home. That home is your church.

Where You Run For Help!

Your church is the first and foremost place you need to run in times of need. Unfortunately, it seems that throughout time, in a naturally narcissistic culture, the church has become the last.

Verse 17 says, "when he came to his senses." In other words, if he's just now coming to his senses, then it implies that up to this point he hasn't been thinking very clearly. He's made dumb decisions. He's made selfish decisions. He's not thinking straight. Up to this point, his desire was to dissociate himself from his family. Isn't that exactly how we treat God so often in our lives? We want the perks of being a Christian but we don't want to associate with His family. I hear story after story from folks who accepted Jesus but then fell away. But, one day you "came to your senses" and you realized that home is the place where you ought to be.

Where do you run for help? When you've made a mistake what's your first instinct? When you've screwed up, do you run away from the church or do you run towards the church? Are you teachable enough to "come back to your senses"? Do you realize that you don't have to define yourself by those mistakes because your identity is still in tact? Your identity determines your destiny, not your mistakes.

This is why you need a church to call your home. A good church home is where you'll receive unconditional love which is exactly what this prodigal son received from his father. Check out the next verse...

> So he got up and went to his father. "But while he was still a long way off, his father saw him and was filled with compassion for him; he ran to his son, threw his arms around him and kissed him. (Luke 15:20)

Now, as if it's not amazing enough that this father was filled with compassion as it says, you need to understand that in old-school Jewish culture, fathers like this would never run for any reason whatsoever. His son would have been perfectly content just being one of his father's servants. Rather he was treated like royalty when he returned home. In fact, his father didn't stop by just welcoming his son home. He then instructed that a robe be put on his son and a ring on his finger.

I'm sure in our modern-day world, a ring seems rather insignificant. But back in their day, the father would often wear a ring which was specifically designed for his family. It was his family seal, if you will. When he wrote a letter, that letter would be sealed with imprinted candle-wax. Do you know where that imprint came from? Typically, from the ring he wore. This father didn't just slide any old ring on his son's finger. He transferred his identity back to his son.

You need a home where you can receive encouragement instead of discouragement. A place where you can receive comfort rather than criticism. A place where there are people who help you rather than tear you down. That's called unconditional love.

Where You Grow Up...

At some point or another, you have to grow up. If you don't grow up at home, what's gonna happen when you go out into the world?

The world is gonna eat you up. We've all heard the story where a student graduates and goes off to college or maybe into the military. You think they're ready only to find that the world just scarfs them right up.

Maybe that was you.

If you'd had a church home, would that have made a difference? Maybe you need a church home now.

Here's what I believe. I believe that just like your home where you physically grew up should have also been the place where you matured as a person, your church should be your home where you spiritually grow up. That way when you go out into the real world, you don't get eaten alive!

Obviously, the prodigal son took his inheritance and left. He did not grow up, until he came to his senses. He had to go through the hard times on his own. He had to learn things the hard way. You see, if you don't make the effort to grow up, eventually you're going to fall down!

**If you don't make the effort to grow up...
eventually you're going to fall down!**

Those who don't grow up spiritually and remain immature will not live lives of significance. How would you answer this question, "Would you rather be successful or would you rather be significant?" You see, immature people seek only after success, whereas the spiritually mature people seek to be significant! Success is temporary. Significance can make a difference for eternity. I believe that God wants to make you significant.

Where You Find Your Identity...
As you find your home in your church you'll also begin to find your identity. You'll begin to discover whom God made you to be and become. The father of the prodigal son puts a robe on him. He puts a ring on his finger. He throws a party for him. He completely ignores the mistakes that his son made. He refuses to allow his son to define himself by those mistakes and he allows his son, once again, to find his identity by coming home. In fact, the father says this...

> *For this son of mine was dead and is alive again; he was lost and is found.' So they began to celebrate.* (Luke 15:24)

The father says, "this son of mine." It's important for you to understand that this boy never ceased to be this father's son. No matter what decisions he made, he was still his father's son. I want you to know that no matter what you've done and no matter where you come from, you are still your Father's child! The unfortunate thing is that as you stray away from your church family, most likely you'll forget that point. You need a church home!

But The Church Is Flawed!
Indeed it is!

It's flawed because it's full of a bunch of flawed people. Like me. I'm flawed and I lead a church. (Boy are we in trouble!)

My family loves reminiscing and sharing memories. They love telling a story that I can't remember (therefore I doubt there's any truth to it!). I was a young child and evidently my older sister upset me. (That much I can believe!) Now, I don't want you to misunderstand me. I love my older sister, but like any sibling, she must have really ticked me off. Do you know how I responded? I responded by walloping her across the head with a baseball bat. (Just to be clear, she didn't get my physical height. She's about as tall as a t-ball stand. So, I can totally justify taking a swing at her head!)

Another story we love to share is one I can remember. My older sister and I waited patiently in the back seat of the car while Mom and Dad searched for a new car roaming the parking lot. One thing led to another and before I knew what had happened, my sister had stabbed my hand with a key. She didn't just cut my hand. There was a key literally sticking out of my hand perpendicular to my skin. (I still have the scar to prove it!)

Now, here's what I want you to understand. Even though my family had moments like those, I grew up in a strong, healthy, Christian home. My dad was an elder in the church. I can remember him preaching when the pastor was on vacation. Do you know that family who is at church every time the doors are unlocked? Yeah, that was us! I simply cannot fully put into words how amazing my family is. So, why would we have those kinds of stories to tell today? Because like every close family, there's still conflict. We still had problems. We still had drama, arguments, hurt feelings and toes that were stepped on. That's family, right!? While I took a whack at my sister with a baseball bat, when we set foot on the school bus the next morning, you better not touch my sister 'cause I'll take you out! In my opinion, that's the way family should be.

That's exactly how a healthy church should operate as well. Here's the trap that I've seen our modern culture fall into. Sure, I want my church to feel like a family. That sounds nice until we truly begin to dissect how a healthy family operates. All we want are the good times. We don't want the drama and disagreement. Once someone takes a swing at someone else, we begin to think this must not be a healthy church. Once that determination has been made, we go searching for a new church family. I see this happen over and over again. The problem isn't that we have an improper definition of what the church should be. The problem is our improper definition of the family.

The question is not IF there will be conflict. The question is how the church will respond when conflict arrises. A healthy church knows that there is going to be conflict. That's one of the key differences between a healthy church and an unhealthy church. They don't sweep the conflict under the rug. Rather, they deal with it as needed.

Your New Home...

Searching for a church home causes a great amount of anxiety even for the seasoned Christian, but finding a church you can call home will be pivotal in your journey with Christ. I wish I could tell you specifically how to know when a church is "home" or not. But you'll know. At Christ's Church, our core values are centered on making church feel like home. In everything we say and do, we want to be "Real, Relevant and Relational." We want a place of safety where you feel comfortable regardless of your background. We want to cultivate a vibe of acceptance regardless of your skin color or how much money you may or may not have in your bank account. We want an environment that's not judgmental regardless of what may be in your past. We want an environment where you know you are welcome. Unfortunately, not every church will strive after that same atmosphere. The fact is this, many churches still show favoritism.

Please don't hear me wrong. In no way am I attempting to portray Christ's Church as perfect or even better than others. We have plenty of problems ourselves. But, the most segregated hour in America throughout the entire week is still 11:00am on Sunday morning. Why? Well, because that's the most common church service time. We recently had a black couple begin attending who tried out many churches in our community. While attending one black-gospel church, they asked the pastor why there were not any white people at that church. The pastor responded,

"White people go to white churches and black people go to black churches."

That breaks my heart.

I believe that breaks God's heart too!

The fact is this, there is only one heaven. That one heaven will have blacks and whites and every ethnicity from around the world. It will have every denomination represented. And, I'm guessing, you might even meet some folks you didn't think you'd see. Our earthly churches would do well to try and emulate that.

At Christ's Church, we have also changed our terminology when it comes to membership. We do not have church members. Rather, we have church partners. There's nothing wrong with any churches who prefer to call those who join their church, "members." It's just our preference to use the term "partner."

One local pastor recently wanted to make that a debate with me. Using the Apostle Paul's words of how we are all members of one body. He's has a point...

> *For just as each of us has one body with many members, and these members do not all have the same function, so in Christ we, though many, form one body, and each member belongs to all the others.* (Romans 12:4-5)

It does seem that Paul is directing us to all be "members of one body." However, I don't know that he was as concerned about the terminology as he was about unity in the church! To use this passage as concrete and "physical" doctrine to support your terminology is trivial. By his logic then, we should all be physically joined at the hip.

I love you.

Just not quite that much.

Here's why we call those who join our church "partners." One definition for member is "a person who belongs to a club, political party, etc." In other words, members have rights. I believe I referred to a passage earlier about taking up your cross daily. In essence, that means you are giving up your rights.

Have you ever experienced the church where a member tithes and then feels because he's a tithing member that he deserves certain rights? For the first twelve years of my ministry in the local church, I served as a worship pastor. I love music and I love leading people before God's throne in worship, but, I can remember in one church when an individual approached me. He politely informed me that he was a tithing member of this church. And as a tithing member of this church, I needed to sing the song he wanted me to sing.

Um... if that's what tithing means to you... we have deeper issues!

He didn't want to talk about that.

I didn't sing his song!

God did not design his church to function like a country club full of stuck-up Christians demanding their rights. (Yes, I'm on a little soapbox now!) Because of this mentality, many churches today are suffering from their buildings being filled with consumers rather than contributors. A consumer is one who attends worship services on the weekend but does nothing else. They don't get involved in church life throughout the week and they don't offer their time and talents for the cause of Christ.

On the other hand, a contributor does not just attend the church services, he or she also contributes - hence the name. By eliminating the word "member" from our culture, we've been able to help some of the consumers find their place as contributors.

Rather than using the word "member," we now call those who join the church "partner." Check out the definition of partner... "a person associated with another or others on a joint venture, usually sharing its risks and profits."[11] That's the kind of church I want to be

---

11 Dictionary.com, 2a, accessed March 01, 2015, http://dictionary.reference.com/browse/partner?s=t.

a part of - one where everyone comes together on a joint venture. I believe that's the way God dreams for his local church to function here on earth.

You Can't Make It By Yourself...

I love watching Clydesdale horses. I don't know what it is about seeing them trot down a road all in unison pulling a large load behind them. A single Clydesdale horse can grow to be over six feet tall and weigh as much as 2,400 pounds. It's reported that one horse can single-handedly pull approximately three times its own body weight.

That's impressive.

Any idea what two horses can pull together? Logic would say twice as much, right? But it's actually so much more. In fact, if one horse weighs 2,000 pounds and is coupled with another 2,000 pound horse, together they can pull approximately 18,000 pounds. Pretty amazing! That's why we call it *horsepower!*

That's exactly what the Apostle Paul was talking about in Romans. I don't know that he was as concerned about the word we use for those who have joined the church as much as he was concerned about them having unity. Paul was attempting to get across the point that we all have different abilities and different gifts. Alone you can make a difference. However, when you partner with others, that difference becomes exponentially greater.

Whether a church has members or partners, or whatever terminology they choose to use, you need to find a church and officially join that community of believers. You need to make it official and begin to lay down roots in that local community of believers. And you need to begin to use your gifts and talents to make a difference in combination with the other believers in that church.

What Did Jesus Die For?

I want to give you one final thought before we continue. It took me years to pick up on this. You may already know this. I'm a simple guy and sometimes I don't notice the details.

Did you know that Jesus didn't just die for you? Sure, that's one of the big reasons. We're taught the most popular verse in the Bible from a very early age...

> *For God so loved the world that he gave his one and only Son, that whoever believes in him shall not perish but have eternal life.* (John 3:16)

So, yes, Jesus died on the cross for you. But he also died for something else. Check this out...

> *Husbands, love your wives, just as Christ loved the church and gave himself up for her to make her holy cleansing her by the washing with water through the word, and to present her to himself as a radiant church, without stain or wrinkle or any blemish, but holy and blameless.* (Ephesians 5:25-27)

Jesus didn't just die for you.

He also died for his church.

In other words, you cannot love Jesus and not love his church. Because the church is managed and full of flawed people, the church is flawed, as we've already spoken about. And because the church is flawed, we have used that as our excuse to not be involved with a local church. So, let me ask you one quick question. If Jesus died on the cross for the church, do you think His church might be important enough that you be a part of it?

How To Connect To A Church...

I want to be very clear and intentional to give you a healthy explanation of what it looks like to connect with a local church in your community. However, I think the best way is to first explain what it does not look like.

I wish I knew the reasons for why the modern church is in the state that it's in. But, I do not. All I can share is my experience. The majority of people who walk through our church doors on Sunday morning, sit down, observe, and then walk away. For most of them, that is the extent of their connection.

Maybe they feel as though they've accomplished their weekly duty.

Maybe it's a routine.

Maybe it's a ritual.

Maybe it's a tradition.

All of the above are how we would define religion. I've also found that many people are very religious. Religion, though, is merely a bunch of laws and policies stating what you can and cannot do.

As you skim through the four Gospel accounts in the Bible, you'll find some very religious people. They were called the Pharisees. In fact, they were so focussed on the religious laws that they were more concerned about following the rules than truly making a difference in the lives of others. On top of that, they were so focussed on the rules that they failed to focus on their relationship. What we've forgotten is that you can be religious and still lack a relationship!

—⚍—

You can be religious and still lack a relationship!

—⚍—

You can do all the right things. You can say all the right words. You can sing all the right songs. You can raise your hands during the chorus and close your eyes during the verse. You can give your money. You can do all the right things and know a whole lot about Jesus and the Bible, yet still lack a relationship with him.

God Made You For More...
I believe God made you for more than just attending a Sunday morning church service. I believe that God designed you with a very specific purpose in mind. And I believe that God desires for you to discover how he designed you and then begin to make a difference for him. How do you do that? First, you serve.

I'm going to assume that if you're still reading by this point that you have a deep desire to grow more and more like Christ. That's a big goal. And there are all kinds of characteristics we find in the bible of how we should be like Christ. For example...

> *Not so with you. Instead, whoever wants to become great among you must be your servant, and whoever wants to be first must be your slave - just as the Son of Man did not come to be served, but to serve, and to give his life as a ransom for many. (Matt. 20:26-28)*

In other words, if Jesus came not to be served but to serve, then it's a spiritual impossibility for you to become *Christlike* apart from developing a servant's heart. I believe the best place for you to do that is in your local church.

Serving connects you with others in your church.
Serving enables you to make a difference in the lives of others.
Serving grows you into a more mature follower of Christ.

If you are not serving in your local church, stop making excuses and get plugged in. It's one of the key and critical components to defeating drift in your life. I'll talk more about serving in a while.

CHAPTER 4

Defeating The Drift: Connecting With Others

I can remember growing up in Indiana. My Mom's family were farmers. As a young boy, I loved going over to the farm. Grandpa farmed all kinds of things from animals to fields. They raised cattle, pigs, and chickens. They grew corn and peas, tomatoes and potatoes. You name it and they probably tried to grow it at one time or another.

Meal time was the best at Grandma & Grandpa's house because whatever they grew... they ate! Grandma would bring out these massive platters with heaping piles of corn on the cob (which Grandpa taught me how to put down in record-breaking time), giant plates of homegrown tomatoes, and a huge pot roast with potatoes. To call it a feast would be an understatement.

Somewhere along the line I developed something which still characterizes me to this day. As a matter of fact, I am still made fun of it to this day. I'm not sure how it developed, but it did. You might be able to can relate. You see, somewhere throughout my life I developed this habit of compartmentalizing my food. Do you do that? Maybe you do not, but I would bet you at least know someone who does. See, not only do I have a certain order that I have to eat my food in, but on top of that, none of my food can touch either. No touchy, touchy! No crossing the boundaries. No mixing. No concoctions. No stirring things up. If God would have wanted us to mix up our food, I'm sure he would have created it to come out of the fields like that. That's my philosophy.

I also always save what I like the best for last, which I know I should eat first because I probably wouldn't eat as much (It doesn't matter how full I am, I'm eating that fried chicken, okay!) But, I'm just saying, what's even worse is when your food runs together. I can remember being so frightened as I watched my grandpa take his mashed potatoes, corn and gravy and mix 'em all up together. (By the way, that's where Kentucky Fried Chicken got their Famous Bowl ideas). That's just gross. I know it's all going to the same place. But that's just me. I compartmentalize my eating. I'm even so obsessive that at potluck dinners at church, the plate that I go for is the one that has 3 or 4 different sections with walls, that way I can have boundaries built up between my food.

Are you like that?

No?

Well, that's not normal to stir everything up!

You realize that we do exactly the same thing throughout our lives when it comes to relationships? A few of you don't have any problems. You mix everything up. Most of us, though, would look at you and say, "Man, that is not normal." Because most of us prefer that plate with the walls so that we can have those natural boundaries built up between us which enables us to compartmentalize our relationships.

I believe that one of the missing links in today's church is solid Christian relationships. As a matter of fact, I believe those relationships are absolutely critical to the health of the church, because your relationships drive both what is normal and what is possible in your life!

Your relationships drive both what is normal and what is possible in your life!

In other words, it is through the lens of your relationships that you view the rest of the world. It is through your relationships that you differentiate normal from abnormal. Whether you realize it or not, we all do this. It doesn't matter where you are in your faith journey with Christ, you do this exact thing.

It is also through the power and strength of your relationships that you discover possibilities in your life. If you're walking around throughout this life as a spiritual zombie then your natural instinct is going to be to isolate yourself, to fend for yourself, to place yourself as the priority in your life, rather than God.

The Apostle Paul wrote a letter a long, long time ago to a group of people who called themselves the church in Ephesus. This was a real church like our churches today. It was a group of believers attempting to follow Christ with all of their lives and reaching as far into their community as they possibly could. This church is also one of the seven churches mentioned in Revelation, the final book of the Bible.

As Jesus addresses this church he commends them for their good deeds. He praises them for their dedication and their commitment. However, he gives them a little nudge and talks about how they have lost their *first love*. See, the folks in the church of Ephesus were all "doing" the right things. They were "saying" all the right words. They were singing all the right worship songs, praying all the right prayers and preaching all the right sermons. The problem was that their hearts were not in it. Their passion and their joy had all been lost. Jesus basically tells them that a church without heart is a church without life. In other words, they were zombies! They had lost their reason for existing. They had lost touch with their mission and purpose as a church.

Living With A Cause...

Let me ask you a few questions. What is your cause? What is the purpose for your existence? What do you want to accomplish in your life? What is the legacy you want to leave behind? (Okay that was, like, four questions.) Has it ever occurred to you that the ones you hang around with will drive your cause? They will drive your reason for existence.

For example, if you hang out with a bunch of folks who are always talking about creating the next best thing and making it rich you will find yourself quickly consumed with the next get-rich-quick scheme. If you hang around folks who always talk about winning the lottery, you'll quickly find that getting rich has become your cause in life.

If you hang out with folks who don't really care about anyone or anything but themselves you'll quickly begin to think as they do. Hang out with folks who love the homeless and you just may develop a heart for the homeless as well.

However, hang out with folks who have huge, giant, honking vision and guess what you'll start seeing. Seeing a huge vision will seem normal to you. And, those without vision will begin to seem abnormal. You get the point, right?

Your relationships mold your reason. They will mold your perception of possibilities. They will drive the cause for which you live. Your relationships will forge how you think and morph your outlook on life. So, what's your cause? What are you living for? What's your purpose? I've heard Rick Warren, author of the best-selling book *The Purpose Driven Life*, say that you were made by God and for God and until you understand that, life will never make sense. The Apostle Paul said it like this...

> *For this cause I bow my knees unto the Father of our Lord Jesus Christ...* (Eph. 3:14)

I don't know how you felt this morning when you woke up. But I do know this... Satan wants to kill your cause. He wants to shut you down. Do you know why? Because Satan knows that just like the church in Ephesus, a church without heart is a church without life... and a church without life is a church full of spiritual zombies. Satan wants you to doubt. He wants you to question your cause.

Can I just fill you in on something?

I don't know if you've realized this yet or not, but you are not an accident. You were not accidentally created. God has never made and accident. He never will.

You are not an accident!

I don't know if you can fully comprehend that or not. But, you need to know that you are NOT an accident. You need to know that God knew exactly what He was doing when He formed you in your mother's the womb. God knew exactly what he was doing when He created you. Paul talks about that towards the beginning of Ephesians in...

> *Even before he made the world, God loved us and chose us in Christ to be holy and without fault in his eyes. 5 God decided in advance to adopt us into his own family by bringing us to himself through Jesus Christ.* (Eph. 1:4-5)

Allow me to take this one step further. Since God knew you before you were ever born, that means that God knew every great thing you would ever do in this life. God was fully aware of every joke you would ever make that would make others laugh. He was fully aware of every act of kindness you would do to help someone else. God was also fully aware of how you would fail in this life. He was fully aware of every sin you would commit. And even though you'll screw things up in this life, God still allowed you to be born.

You are not an accident!
You have a purpose in this life!
You were born to do great things!

But, here's the thing. When you stop hanging out with God and other followers of Christ, Satan will get inside of your head and your heart and cause you to doubt your cause! However, when you hang out with other solid followers of Christ, you'll be surrounded by those who will help you fight off those times of doubt. Let me show you how dangerous life can be when you continue to live alone.

Accidental Drift...

If you've ever been to the beach and swam in the ocean, I'm confident you've experienced what most people have. (It's really what this entire book is about.) You walk out on the beach and set up camp. You have the lawn chairs, the towels, the umbrella, the ice chest. You name it, you got it. So, you set everything up and go running for the water. You're swimming. You're body surfing. You might even walk on water if you feel something brush up against your leg. Suddenly you look up only to find that your belongings moved. Your first thought is you got robbed. But then you realize what really happened. Your belongings didn't move. You moved. That's what I call accidental drift. It happens to everyone at the beach who's not intentional. See, the only alternative to accidental drift is intentionality!

The only alternative to accidental drift is intentionality!

Here's my point. If you're not intentional in your new journey with Christ, you'll drift. Plain and simple. You can continue trying to convince yourself that you're stronger than the waves that will pound up against you, but you're not. You'll go back to work on Monday and continue to live in the same way you did before. You'll go back to school and still give in to peer pressure. The only way to guarantee you make it from point A to point B is by living an intentional life.

When I was growing up it wasn't uncommon to see a high school senior graduate fall away from his life with Christ by the end of his freshman year of college. I was just told the other day that now it takes less than six weeks into his freshman year on average. Statistically, that's how quickly one can drift.

Learn from those who have gone before you. Learn from the choices they've made. Let me give you two primary keys to preventing accidental drift in your life.

Accidental Drift Key #1...

Have you ever realized how you adapt to the people around you? If you know me then you know that I am an extreme introvert. I could sit in my office all day long with no human interaction and be perfectly fine. However, take me out of that office and place me face to face across the lunch table with someone I've never met and I'm petrified. My wife is the complete opposite. (She completes me!) She could have a logical conversation with a brick wall for three hours and not think anything of it. I, on the other hand, freeze up.

But, here's what I've noticed. When I hang out with my extroverted friends, suddenly I feel this swell of confidence begin to ooze through my veins. When I first began in ministry and needed to visit someone in the hospital whom I've never met, I always took my extroverted wife along with me. Having her by my side made all the difference in the world. I knew if I didn't know what to say that she'd pick up my slack. Can you imagine how awkward that visit would have been had I taken an introvert along with me?

Here's my point. It doesn't matter who you are or how strong you think you may be, you will begin to conform to the likeness of the people on your left and your right. You will begin to adjust your lifestyle to meet theirs. Therefore, with whom you surround yourself is of the utmost importance in your life.

That's why you need to be involved in a small group in your church. A small group of what, you ask? A small group of people whom you will learn to call your "peeps." Many churches have their own version of small groups. My goal isn't to explain different models. Rather, my goal is to simply convince you to be involved. Whether it's a group that meets in someone's home throughout the week or a group you meet with on Sunday mornings, you won't make it alone.

Your small group is more than just a weekly Bible study. Your small group is your family. If you live somewhere away from your biological family, your small group will become your family away from your family. They will become your best friends. They will care for you in your times of deepest need and, likewise, you'll care for them. You'll grow so close to those in your small group that they'll be the first ones you call to go out to dinner or to the movies. I've even seen small groups go on vacation together.

Mine did.

Can you guess what we did?

We went on a cruise!

I can remember several years ago receiving a call from my mother late at night. Mom was calling to let me know that Dad had an accident with his table saw. He was trying to cut a beveled piece of wood that would create a ramp needed to roll around other large power tools in his shop from one level to another. Cutting bevels like that requires you to change the angle of the saw blade on your table saw which makes the blade much closer to your fingers. As Dad was pushing the block of wood through the saw the blade began to pull at his left hand. His thumb was fine, but he lost his left index finger down to the second knuckle and his other three fingers down to the their first knuckles. Mom rushed him to the emergency room.

Can you guess what happened that night?

If you've ever been part of a small group, I bet you can.

If you haven't been part of a small group, then you're robbing yourself!

My parents were part of a small group of "seasoned" folks in their church. (That's the politically correct way to describe "old" right?) About 10:00 pm (when they all should be in bed), every person from their small group came walking into the ER to be with Mom and Dad. The doctor thought they were having a party.

Over the next several weeks, my parents' small group took care of their every need. They brought them food. They mowed their grass. They took Dad back to the doctor. You name it, they were there. That's the power of a small group.

My parents have moved since that time and no longer live close to those folks. But, fortunately with today's technology, they've kept those friendships in tact and strong.

You have two choices in this life. You can surround yourself with other Christian friends and remain strong. Or, you can surround yourself with non-Christians and... well, you get the point. So, here's the question. Who's on your left and who's on your right?

Accidental Drift Key #2...

I am a huge football fan. I can't keep all of the names of the famous players straight (mainly cause I'm old and have lost my memory). But I love to watch the game. Because I was born in Indiana, I was born a Colts fan! I also love Peyton Manning, arguably one of the greatest quarterback to have ever played the game. I follow him on the Broncos, but I'm still a die hard Colts fan first and foremost.

Do you know what I love about the game? I love the team aspect. This isn't one-on-one tennis or golf. If you want to win at football then you need a team. Not only do you need a team, you also need those on your team playing the role that they play best.

Can you imagine if Peyton Manning also had to double up playing wide receiver? I know some quarterbacks are pretty fast. But none exist with the capability to throw the ball and then run down the field to catch it. If that were the expectation, Peyton Manning would go from being one of the best quarterbacks to being one of the worst. Or, can you imagine your punter as a defensive lineman? You can have the right people on your team, but if you have them playing the wrong positions, you'll struggle to win!

Sadly, too many churches are operating with a similar philosophy. They have good people. But they're serving in the wrong areas. Serving in the sweet spot of your life is the second key to preventing accidental drift.

When you discover how God wired you and what gifts he's given you and then you use those gifts to make a difference, you will begin to find personal fulfillment like never before. The key, however, is discovering your gifts. There are many different assessment tests which can aid you in this discovery (not to be confused with a test you can pass or fail. In fact, you can find several online for free. Just do a search online for "Spiritual Gifts Assessment.") Once you discover your God-given spiritual gifts and begin to couple those gifts with your passions, it's like combining a couple Clydesdale horses together. You will accomplish great things. Combined with others, you can accomplish exponentially better things! Let me give you an example.

One of my top spiritual gifts is teaching. I have a passion for 20-somethings and college-age. In the past, when I led a small group of 20-somethings, I couldn't wait for that night each week when we'd meet. In fact, I looked forward to that time more than I did Sundays. I was effective at teaching them not only because I have the spiritual gift of teaching but also because I have a passion for them.

On the other hand, consider if I were asked to teach a group of elementary children on a Sunday morning. I have a child of my own. I love her and would give my life for her. However, I'm allergic to every other child on the planet. Could I teach those children? Sure. Would I do a good job? Sure. Would I enjoy it and be personally fulfilled? Nope! That's the difference between utilizing your gifts and passions and just doing a job. If you're volunteering outside of your gifts and passion areas, you'll dread every time you're scheduled to serve. You'll dread your alarm going off on Sunday mornings. You'll dread church and you might even come to resent it altogether. However, when you use your gifts and your passions, now you can't wait to serve. You'll make a much larger impact for the kingdom and you'll be much more personally fulfilled doing it.

Everybody Can Play A Part...
I love this passage the Apostle Paul wrote describing how we are all to work together within the church for the cause of Christ.

> *But in fact God has placed the parts in the body, every one of them, just as he wanted them to be.* (1 Cor. 12:18)

In other words, God created you to be the person you are. You're not an accident and God has a plan for you. It's your job to figure it out. It's your responsibility to take your passions, your talents and your gifts, and put them all together to discover how God can use you. It doesn't matter who you are, God can use you! Everybody can play a part. When you play your part and I play my part, there is nothing that can stop us from accomplishing God's desires for us.

What is it you were created to do? Unlike me, maybe you have a passion for children. You understand that if our children are not taught about Jesus, odds are that they will never accept Him as their savior the rest of their lives. If that's your gifting and passion, then use it! Maybe you love serving along side of middle school or high school students. If you've ever been with a student when the "light" came on, that's a pretty amazing feeling! Maybe you are an extreme extrovert. You love interacting with people. Why not greet them at the front door as they enter and help them feel comfortable?

Do you know what happens so often in the church? When people begin to fade off of ministry teams, often, it's because they've begun to see their service as menial. They don't see the difference they're making and they fail to understand that every task is a spiritual task!

—w—

Every task is a SPIRITUAL task!

—w—

Parking cars is a spiritual task!
Brewing coffee is a spiritual task!
Mowing grass, painting walls, handing out programs... are all spiritual tasks.

We may begin to think that the only one doing the spiritual things is the preacher or the one leading worship. Listen, every task is a spiritual task! Folding and stuffing the programs is a spiritual task. Turning off the A/C, locking the doors and taking out the trash after the services are all spiritual tasks because they enable more people to feel more comfortable at church. That's the potential God placed within you. Can you imagine the difference you can make in the lives of others by simply discovering your gifts and passions and then offering to use them?

There's another added benefit to using your gifts, though. Most people can learn through good preaching. They can learn through their own personal Bible study. They can learn by participating in a small group as well. However, you will not grow past a certain point if you're not involved in serving others. As I mentioned earlier, you simply cannot become like Christ apart from developing a servant's heart. By not serving, you are placing a glass ceiling over your head and restricting yourself. As a matter of fact, the more you put into church the more you'll get out of church!

**The more you put into church...
the more you'll get out of church!**

Are you ready to jump into that cycle? Put in... get out. Remove that lid that's been hanging over your life preventing you from your next step in your faith journey. Get plugged into a small group. Get plugged into serving at your church. Defeat the drift in your life!

CHAPTER 5

Defeating The Drift: Achieving Financial Control

I'm just gonna get something right out in the open. I love money!
I love how it makes me feel. I love to spend it. I love how it makes me appear before others who don't have as much as I do. I love to give it away (as long as I still have enough for me). I love money.

Do you love money too?

Here's the thing, though. Since serving in the local church, I've learned that for most Christians, the number one thing that is preventing them from taking their next step in their faith journey is money. It doesn't have anything to do with how much or how little you may have. However, it does have everything to do with how you manage what's in your possession. For most, a paradigm shift is required.

Life is full of all kinds of paradigm shifts. Have you ever noticed that? A paradigm shift can be defined as *"a radical change in underlying beliefs or theory."*[12] For example, when you were younger every girl hated boys and every boy hated girls. Boys had cooties and girls were gross. But as each year came and went, you became intrigued

---

12 Dictionary.com, section goes here, accessed March 01, 2015, http://dictionary.reference.com/browse/paradigm+shift.

by those horrid creatures. You began to see them differently. That's a paradigm shift in your perspective.

Or, most of us couldn't wait to get our driver's license growing up. You wanted to get your own car. You thought it would rocket you straight up to the top of the "popular" category in high school. Then you got your license and you realized that driving isn't really all that special after all. Once you have your own car, that brings along a whole new set of responsibilities in life.

For some of you, you couldn't wait to graduate high school. You longed for independence. You couldn't wait to be on your own; make your own decisions; tackle life on your own without anyone looking over your shoulder. Then, you moved out on your own only to wish you could move back. (Some of you did.)

Last example. How about this? Forever and ever you wanted a baby. You wanted a daughter with big bows in her hair. You wanted a son so the two of you could go fishing. Then the baby was born and after 48 hours with no sleep, you were ready to give the thing back.

This life is full of all kinds of paradigm shifts, but there is one paradigm shift that most never make. In my opinion, without a shadow of a doubt, it is the most important paradigm shift you could ever make in your thinking and outlook on life. I'm telling ya, if you make this shift in your thinking, your life will never be the same. Your marriage will never be the same. As elementary as it may sound, if our government made this change, our country would never be the same. This one little tiny paradigm shift is one that could literally change the world.

Stephen Covey once said that the way we see things is the source of the way we think and the way we act.[13] That's where the paradigm shift comes in. A paradigm shift is that moment of clarity when you realize there's an entirely different way of seeing things than the way you've always seen them.

---

13 "A Quote by Stephen R. Covey," Goodreads, section goes here, accessed March 01, 2015, https://www.goodreads.com/quotes/720041-the-way-we-see-things-is-the-source-of-the.

Are you ready for the shift?
Are you ready to defeat the financial drift in your life?
Here we go!

I Want You To Win...

Because of my financial decisions, I have experienced going through life financially strapped. Also because of my financial decisions, I have experienced living financially free. Now, I'm not debt free. That would be nice. I'm working towards that. When I say financially free, I'm talking about getting to the point in your lifestyle where you are in control of your money rather than allowing your money to be in control of you. Unfortunately, most Americans would have to admit that their money controls them.

One of my deepest desires for you is to win with your money. I want you to know what it's like to live in complete financial freedom. At the same time, though, I also know that it takes a little grit to get to that point. The main reason is because the number one competitor for your heart is money. Don't worry, it is for me as well. It is for everyone.

It seems that we have allowed money to define who we are. Consequently, money is now one of the foremost reasons cited for divorce. It's one of the top reasons for stress and anxiety. I'm afraid your financial situation has much more of an impact on you than you'll ever fully know. And at the core of the issue lies one question... Who's #1 in your life?

Who's #1 in your life?

Really this entire book comes down to that one question. One of the most prevalent areas we have to ask this question in is the area of finances.

Have you ever noticed your mental and emotional state when you have extra money? If you're like me, here's what happens. Let's say I get some extra money for Christmas, or maybe a gift card or two. In that moment, there's a switch that flips inside of me. I'm not a shopper by any stretch of the means, but suddenly I'm feeling the urge to go. When I have extra money, I can't wait for Christmas to be over so I can go shopping the next day. I tend to become a geek as I usually want to spend it on some sort of gadget or technology.

You know the feeling, right? That's what money does to us on an emotional level because money magnifies who you already are!

Money magnifies who you already are!

I don't know why. I don't know how. Money always brings out who we are deep down inside. And as it does, we tend to make dumb decisions.

My Dumbest Financial Decision Ever...

I'll be vulnerable with you for a minute. Here's how stupid I am. This isn't just stupid. This is beyond stupid. And I'm still kicking myself in the rear for this. There was a family in one of the churches I served that Amanda & I got really close to. They were a very wealthy family. Unlike me, they had made very wise financial decisions and honored God with their wealth. In return, God blessed them more.

One year for Christmas the husband in this family bought his wife a new Mercedes. They didn't trade in their old vehicle so they had an extra car sitting in their driveway. I was driving around an old Honda Civic with 250,000 miles and no A/C. (Which in Florida is stinking hot!) A few weeks later, here they came driving up into my driveway in their 2004, near mint-condition, Lincoln Navigator. It looked like it had just been driven off the car lot. They handed me an envelope with the title and said, "Here, we want you to have this." Inside of the envelope was also a check for $1000 to get it registered. They said that they didn't care if we kept it or sold it. It was ours to do with however we chose.

I had some bills that I really wanted to get paid off so I decided to sell the car. Got $23,000 for it. Not too shabby, huh! Paid off the bills, which was smart. Bought me a Nissan Maxima with cash. That was smart, too. So, I'm on a roll being smart with my money.

Do you remember me mentioning earlier, though, about being a geek and loving gadgets? Let's just say that I bought a few. I bought my wife a new camera. Got her a new laptop as well. Got myself a large-screen TV. Before I knew what was going on... poof... presto... wally-bing, wally-bang... all of the money was gone. I'm a dum dum!

Actually, my final act with that money was my grandest of all. I'm talking the grand finale! I took my family to Disney for a week-long vacation. If you've ever been to Disney, you know how they have perfected the technology to suck every last dollar out of your pocket. I'm sure you know how much you can spend in a relatively short amount of time at Disney. We went for a week. We spent so much money that when we got back I had to sell my Nissan Maxima (that I earlier paid cash for) to make up for the difference. In turn, I went to the Volkswagen dealership and got the car that I always wanted and decided to make monthly payments. That was the dumbest financial decision I have ever made. I am gullible.

Have you ever been gullible?

Three Financial Thieves...

One of the things I hate preaching about in church is money. Everybody always gets uncomfortable and squirmy in their seats when the pastor starts to talk about money. I can remember the first time I spoke about money in church, I was scared to death. Then, a few months later, I preached about sex. Let's just say that money is no longer a difficult issue. Just saying.

One of the reasons the church rarely talks about money is because of how the church has been portrayed in the past. I hear it all the time: "*Well, I ain't going to church... cause the church just wants my money.*" And so, the leadership in the church is scared they'll drive people away if they preach God's word and what God says when it comes to managing money.

Here's what I've discovered when I hear people say that the church just wants their money. I've discovered that comment sheds a lot more light on that person's heart than it does about the church itself.

Money was the topic Jesus talked most about when He walked this earth. Jesus knew how gullible we are, so he taught about money more than any other thing. More than love, more than grace, more than forgiveness, more than anything... Jesus spoke about money.

Not convinced yet?

Check this out.

One might think that to *believe* would be a fairly huge topic in the Bible. Apart from believing in God and his Son, Jesus Christ, you have no hope of eternal life. No heaven. No pearly gates. However, the word *believe* is only used in the bible 272 times.

What about the word *pray*? Surely that's a huge theme in scripture. We read time after time when Jesus sought out his Father in prayer. The disciples went to Jesus asking them to teach them how to pray. Paul instructs us to never cease praying. Surprisingly, the word *pray* is only used 371 times in the bible.

One more example. How about the word *love*? That has to be one of the main themes in the bible. Jesus takes all of the laws and commands and boils them down into only two. Love God and love others. Surely that is most important. Still, the word *love* is only used 714 times.

Any guess as to how often we find the word *give*? Give ourselves. Give our time. Give our money. The word *give* is used 2,161 times in the bible. That's over three times more than love. I don't know about you, but that speaks volumes to me. Maybe there's more to this theme of giving. Maybe because we're gullible. Look at what Jesus says in the Gospel of Matthew:

> 19 *Do not store up for yourselves treasures on earth, where moths and vermin destroy, and where thieves break in and steal. 20 But store up for yourselves treasures in heaven, where moths and vermin do not destroy, and where thieves do not break in and steal. 21 For where your treasure is, there your heart will be also.* (Matthew 6:19-21)

Financial Thief #1: Gullibility!

Have you ever stumbled upon an infomercial? You weren't sure what it was about the advertisement, but you just couldn't turn the channel. The guy talking made all kinds of promises. Just when you were about to turn the channel, he said *"But Wait!"* He doubled the amount of product for the same price. Just pay shipping and handling. You wonder how he knew you were about to change the channel and move on. By the end of the night, you took the bait.

Now, I'm not saying that every product ever sold on TV was a bust. Many are fine. What I'm talking about is the fact that you got *sold*. The same thing happens many times when you go looking for a new car. You walk out with much more than you intended to buy with a much higher monthly payment. That's because we are gullible. Thus, we blame God for not providing for our needs when we're the ones driving up our necessities. We cry out to God to bless us all while we max out our credit cards. Jesus didn't die on the cross to pay off your American Express card. He died on the cross to set you free in *every* area of your life - not just sin and trials and tribulations. I believe he also died to set you free financially.

Jesus said *where your treasure is, there your heart will be also*. He doesn't say in that passage you just read to stop storing up things on earth because it's wrong. He instructed us to not store up those things because they're going to get old. They'll break down. They'll rust. They'll be out of style. Once that happens, you'll just want to buy more.

Whether it's timeshares, make-money-now schemes, or a new set of encyclopedias, we are gullible. Again, there is nothing wrong with any of those things as long as you remain in control of your money and your money does not control you. Once your money takes control, you'll make all kinds of gullible decisions.

Financial Thief #2: Greed!

Why did I go all haywire when I was given that Lincoln Navigator and then sold it for more money than I had ever possessed before in my life? Because of greed. See, at the core of our existence, we are all very self-centered. You have to be or you'll die. You have to feed your hunger when your tummy growls. You have to quench your thirst when your mouth is dry as sand. The problem is that it's really easy to allow those healthy mannerisms to transition into unhealthy ones. Jesus goes on to say...

> No one can serve two masters. Either you will hate the one and love the other, or you will be devoted to the one and despise the other. You cannot serve both God and money. (Matt. 6:24)

No one can serve two masters. You WILL either serve one or the other. It's interesting to me what the two masters listed are. Have you ever thought about this? I would think that Jesus would say you'll either serve God or Satan. What's the opposite of God? Satan, right? That makes sense. But that's not where Jesus goes with this. He says you will either serve God or money. Could Jesus be saying that money is more of a threat to you than Satan? The Apostle Paul said it this way...

> *For the love of money is a root of all kinds of evil. Some people, eager for money, have wandered from the faith and pierced themselves with many griefs.* (1 Tim. 6:10)

Money in and of itself is amoral (i.e, good nor bad). It is what you make it! Money holds the potential to create good or create bad in the one who possesses it! Financial greed will cause major drift in your life! That's because greed is worshipping the resource rather than the Source itself!

—⚌—

Greed is worshipping the resource rather than the source itself.

—⚌—

Please don't hear me wrong. This is not a *be poor for Jesus* book on money. This is not a *if you're rich then you're a sinner* message. This is a *you own the stuff, don't let the stuff own you* message. Jesus is saying, if you serve money, then you won't serve me! But, if you serve me then you won't serve money... money will serve YOU! You can't serve both. Greed has nothing to do with your possessions. Greed is an attitude of the heart.

There are a couple of places that you can easily see greed in someone. One is when you go out to eat somewhere. When you take someone out to eat, you can learn a lot about that person. You see how that person treats the waiter/waitress. You see how they respond when they don't get their soda in a timely manner. You may even see how well they tip. Just ask a waiter/waitress when their least favorite time to work throughout the week is. The majority of them will tell you Sunday afternoon because that's when all the church folks come to eat. They are mean. They are rude. They are cheap tippers. Listen, don't you dare go out to eat after church this Sunday, leave an invite card for your church sitting on the table, and then leave a cheap tip. Use that opportunity to bless that person.

You know where the second area is you can easily see greed? Church! What I've discovered is that most of those cheap tippers from the restaurant also leave cheap tips for God as well. In God's economy that's called being greedy. But there's an even bigger financial thief that gullibility and greed put together. It's fear.

Financial Thief #3: Fear!
I will never forget when my grandmother passed away. I inherited some bedroom furniture along with a few other odds and ends. While I was at her apartment with the rest of the family helping to sort through her belongings, we were overwhelmed with what we found. (I know pastors are known for exaggerating, but this is a true story!) We found in Grandma's freezer over twenty packs of hot dogs. Now, tell me, how long will it take for one, single, elderly lady to eat twenty packs of hot dogs? That's twenty packs times eight hot dogs per pack. That's 160 hot dogs!

But, it didn't stop there. We found forty brand new sticks of deodorant in her bathroom. Now, I'm guessing you didn't know my grandmother personally. You're just gonna have to trust me on this. My Grandma did not have a problem with body odor, okay! There were several other examples of extreme excess we experienced throughout that day. But I'll spare you the details.

I was bewildered. My parents were not. So I asked them what was up with all of the excess. It sure appeared as though Grandma was a greedy old lady, but it was simple. My Grandma lived through the Great Depression. Therefore, for a good portion of her life, whenever something went on sale, she would stock up. Grandma lived her life in fear.

Have you ever been so scared that it caused a weird reaction? In this passage from the Gospel of Matthew, Jesus continues...

> 25 "Therefore I tell you, do not worry about your life, what you will eat or drink; or about your body, what you will wear. Is not life more than food, and the body more than clothes? 33 But seek first his kingdom and his righteousness, and all these things will be given to you as well. 34 Therefore do not worry about tomorrow, for tomorrow will worry about itself. Each day has enough trouble of its own. (Matt. 6:25, 33-34)

Fear is paralyzing isn't it!? When you live like my grandmother, you'll be full of worry. Even though Jesus clearly instructs us to trust him, to lean on him, to not worry. It's difficult when we see the world around us crumble, but check this out...

> Everything in the heavens and earth are yours, O Lord. We adore you as being in control of everything. (1 Chr. 29:11)

If God is truly in control of everything, what do you have to fear? I don't know if you've realized this or not. Fear is one of the most debilitating emotions known to man. Fear is exactly what the Evil One wants you to feel when it comes to your money. And it's a very real emotion. I know what it feels like to give my tithe to the church all while wondering if we'll make it to our next payday. I know what it feels like to withhold my tithe because I'm scared of the position I'll be in should the car break down, for example. Fear will hold you down. If you're going to defeat the financial drift in your life, at some point, you'll need to address your fears.

How To Overcome Financial Fear...
There's only one complete way to fully overcome your financial fear. It's not through saving your money. It's not through retirement. It's not through investing. I'm afraid you might not like the solution. It's actually found in generosity. That's right. The more you give, the less you grip hold of your money. Please know that I'm not suggesting you give everything away and go live under a bridge. I'm talking about intentionally developing a generous heart and blessing others.

Are you intentionally generous?

A while back, my wife and I began giving an allowance to my daughter each payday. Out of that allowance, she has two piggy banks in her room. One is for her tithe and the other for her savings. She can spend the other 80% however she pleases.

What I've noticed, though, is an attitude of expectation. If you have children, I'm guessing you may have experienced this as well. And I have to admit, it's a little irritating to me at times because she doesn't exactly have many chores to justify earning the money. She has to keep her room clean and her bed made. That's pretty much it. Her allowance is basically just a gift... that she now thinks she deserves!

Do you have a similar attitude towards God?

It is so easy for you and I to adopt that same attitude of expectation. And that is absolutely 180 degrees out from what our attitude should be. Rather than an attitude of expectation, we should display an attitude of generosity.

You know what has been really awesome, though, about giving my daughter an allowance? Even though she oftentimes has an attitude of expectation, she still fully understands the *source* of that allowance. That source is ME! Now, go along with me here because you and I know fully well that the source actually is not me. It's God. I only have the money in my hand because of the job with which God has blessed me. I get that. However, that's a little more difficult for her to understand. So, for now, I want her to see me as *the* source. That way as her faith develops, she'll have a very healthy paradigm of who the ultimate source is in her life. So, while she's always asking for things like any normal elementary-aged child, she doesn't have any doubt in her source. She knows that she can rely on me and she's always extremely grateful when we put those few dollars in her hands.

What happens to us as we grow up, leave home, goto college, get our own jobs, buy our own cars, on and on and on? That reliability perspective shifts onto ourselves, right?

Tithing Is Not An Option...

WARNING... DO NOT SKIP THIS SECTION!!! Simply because I used the word *tithing*, you'll be tempted to scoot right on to the next chapter. However, if you only get one thing out of this entire book, this is it. Why? Because if you can wrap your mind around the concept of tithing, every other area of your life will begin to sync up. I wish I could logically explain how it all comes together, but it's a mystery. God oftentimes works in mysterious ways. When you trust God fully enough to tithe, I'm confident that he'll begin to work in mysterious ways in your life. If you want to win with your money in this life... THIS IS IT!!!

Some Christians will claim that God no longer requires us to tithe because tithing is an Old Testament concept. First, it was never a concept. It was a command. Second, do you discount everything in the Old Testament then? When Jesus was born and began his ministry years, he claimed that he did not come to *abolish* the old law. Rather he came to *fulfill* it.

> *17 Do not think that I have come to abolish the Law of the Prophets; I have not come to abolish them but to fulfill them. 18 For truly I tell you, until heaven and earth disappear, not the smallest letter; not the least stroke of a pen, will by any means disappear from the Law until everything is accomplished.* (Matt 5:17-18)

In other words, if you are a follower of Christ, you are still commanded to tithe. We find the foundation of tithing here...

> *"9 You are under a curse - your whole nation - because you are robbing me. 10 Bring the whole tithe into the storehouse, that there may be food in my house. Test me in this,"* says the Lord Almighty, *"and see if I will not throw open the floodgates of heaven and pour out so much blessing that there will not be room enough to store it. 11 I will prevent pests from devouring your crops, and the vines in your fields will not drop their fruit before it is right,"* says the Lord Almighty. (Mal. 3:9-10)

Don't stop reading now.
    You are about to be set free from your fears!
    First, a couple of observations. This passage appears to be telling us that by not tithing, you are robbing God and you are under a curse. Just a thought, here. This is just me. You can take it for what it's worth. I'm not all that sure I want to be cursed by the God of all Creation! Think about it!
    Second, he instructs us to bring the *whole tithe*. You may already know what a tithe is, but I'm not going to make that assumption. In

light of the fact that there's no other arena in our lives that uses the word, I'm gonna break it down. When you go back into the original texts of the bible, a *tithe* is literally ten percent. And not just any ten percent, but the first ten percent. In other words, before you pay any bill, before you get groceries, before you put gas in your car, you are to set aside ten percent to give back to God. Five percent is not a *whole* tithe. That's only half of it. Eight percent is not the *whole* tithe. That's only a portion.

Next, we're instructed to bring the whole tithe into the *storehouse*. When this was written, that would have been the temple. What is the temple in our culture today? Is it not the church? Therefore, we are to bring the first ten percent out of every paycheck to the church to support God's mission through that local church. Some will claim that they give their money to a charity. Or maybe they sponsor a great mission of some sort. However, that's not what we are instructed to do with that first ten percent.

NOW COMES THE GOOD PART.

KEEP READING!!!

We're now told to *test God*. I want you to understand just how huge this is. In fact, out of the sixty-six books in the bible, this is the only time that God gives you permission to test him. In no other area of your Christian life are you challenged to test God. Only with your money. Why? Because God knows that money will always be the number one competitor for your heart!

But, God doesn't stop there. He follows up this challenge with a promise. Don't miss this! He says that if you will honor him and bring that first ten percent to his church, he will *throw open the floodgates of heaven*. Just a little side note. I'm not exactly sure what that means. I'm not sure how much the *floodgates of heaven* could entail. But, in light of the fact that we're told that God has streets made of gold and seas made of crystal... well, you do the math. I'm not saying you're going to win the lottery. I'm not saying if you tithe that you'll walk into work tomorrow to find that you've been given a huge promotion with a corner office. However, I do believe (because I've experienced this personally) that God will begin to take care of your every need.

HOLD ON! There's still more! Next God says that he will *prevent pests from devouring your crops*. But, I'm not a farmer. I don't even have a garden. What is God promising you? God is not only promising you his provision, he's also promising you his protection.

I felt really guilty a couple of years ago when my wife called me after just having been rear-ended in a car accident. You see, we only had three months left to pay on our minivan. (Yes, I'm a minivan man... and I'm cool!) Naturally, my first instinct was to ask if she was okay. However, what followed immediately was my concern about the van. It consumed me. We were on the brink of paying off a huge debt and I really, really, really did not want to be stuck in another car payment for years to come. I almost felt equally concerned about the condition of my van as I was the condition of my wife. I honestly believe that God's hand of protection was upon my wife and upon my minivan that morning. The accident could have been much worse. My wife could have been severely injured, but God protected.

Don't you want God's hand of provision and his hand of protection to be upon your life? I believe the solution is simple. Tithe.

Challenge Accepted...

Remember me saying that I have personally experienced what it's like to live financially stressed and strapped, but now I'm living a life of financial freedom? There's one change that took me from one point to the other. I began to tithe. Please don't view me as a pastor right now just trying to get money. I'm taking off my pastor's hat because I so desperately want you to experience what God has allowed me to experience. The only thing that changed was I began to fully tithe. Furthermore, over the last several years, my wife and

I have been able to increase that percentage to even more than ten percent. So, I want to challenge you today.

Several times per year, I stand before the people of Christ's Church and challenge them to *test God*. I challenge them to take a 3-Month Tithing Challenge. If you'll take the same challenge today, I believe God will transform your life. Here's how it works.

First, you (and your spouse, if you're married) commit to bring the full tithe, your first ten percent of your paycheck to your local church for the next three months. It's okay to tell God that you're testing him because he's already given you permission.

Second, you follow through. As soon as you receive your next paycheck, take that ten percent and give it to your church. If you're like me when I first began to tithe, I didn't wait for Sunday to come. Give online. If your church doesn't have online giving, then write out a check and physically deliver it to the church office. Get it out of the way. Otherwise, you might spend the money by Sunday. We're going to make this a habit in your life!

Next, continue the same process for the next three months and watch God work in your life. Again, I'm not saying that you'll strike oil in your back yard. (If you do, you're welcome!) I'm not saying that a long lost relative will suddenly drop an inheritance in your life. Actually, I've seen quite the opposite happen to folks who step up to this challenge. I've seen them go through hardships, emergencies and unexpected bills. Do you know why? Because Satan is now worried about you. He didn't have to worry about you before because money had a grip on your heart. Now, he has to step up his game. When you take on this challenge you will paint a great big fat bullseye on your back and Satan will open up his arsenal upon you.

Are you encouraged yet?

Hold on!

At Christ's Church, we believe in God's promise so much that we back up the Three-Month Tithing Challenge with a guarantee. In fact, we tell anyone who's willing to take the challenge and begin to tithe the full ten percent for the next three months, if God does not take care of their needs throughout that time then at the end of those three months, we will reimburse them for every penny they gave to the church throughout that challenge. We've been doing this for six years now at the time of this writing. Throughout that time, we've had nearly 600 families take the challenge. Not one has returned after three months asking for their money back. God wants to meet your needs. What he wants more, though, is your heart.

Take the challenge.
Test God.
Watch what happens next!

A Note To Pastors...

First, if you're a pastor and you're not tithing to your church you serve, you should consider whether being a pastor is what you should do in life. If you're not sold out enough to God and to your church to tithe, how can you expect your people to be? Nuff said!

Second, if you have never challenged the people of your church to a Three-Month Tithing Challenge, email me and I will send you a Dropbox link with every resource you need to implement it in your church. Send an email to pastorscott@christschurchcamden.com.

CHAPTER 6

Defeating The Drift: Changing Stories

In February of 2014, I had the opportunity to travel to Kenya with Compassion International. If you're not familiar with Compassion International I would highly recommend you check them out. They are touching the lives of people all around the globe, especially children. My wife and I got to see them in action first hand as we traveled from project to project all around the Nairobi area.

One of the main parts of Compassion's mission is rescuing children from poverty. However, they don't just go into any given community with relief. Rather, their process dives much deeper. Compassion's desire is to develop the local people and, in essence, transform the community or even the country from the inside out. For about the same amount of money per month it would cost to take your family out to eat one time, you can sponsor a child in a foreign country. You pick the child. You pick a boy or girl. You pick where the child is from. Your sponsorship then ensures that your child receives the necessities to survive. Things that most people take for granted, like clean water, medical assistance, education, and clothes. Best of all, your sponsorship ensures that your child gets to meet Jesus. It's very similar to adopting a child in real life.

My family believes in Compassion so much that we sponsor three children. It just so happens that two of them live in Kenya and we had the opportunity to meet them in person while we were there.

That was quite the experience. Little did I know that those two children would do almost anything just to spend two hours of time with me. They had never been to a big city before. They had never ridden on a bus before. They had never even seen white people before (and I'm "vampire" white). They rode on a bus for twelve hours just to spend two hours with my wife and me.

I had envisioned a Hollywood fantasy. All of us running through the wheat field. Wind blowing through our hair (well, through my wife's hair. All of my hair fell out. Too many perms in the 80's!). I saw those adorable little girls jumping into our arms, giving me high fives, blowing up some knuckles. I have to tell you, though, it was nothing like that at all.

Have you ever heard the phrase "Stranger Danger"? That's what we taught my daughter at an early age so that she wouldn't trust strangers. A stranger is what I felt like. They were two of the most adorable girls I had ever seen, but they were scared. And rightly so. As we sat down with the few adults who had accompanied them on the bus ride, we began to eat lunch, and the girls began to open up. They had never seen a camera before. So, to see us take pictures on our smart phones and then have the ability to show them the picture of themselves on the screen, they were very intrigued.

As we ate lunch, I noticed them both continually staring past me. At first, I assumed that it was because I was a stranger. But then I realized something. A short distance behind me was one of those blow-up-bounce houses. It was something that my daughter had seen hundreds of times. However, these two young innocent girls had never experienced the thrill of jumping in one. I wish I could show you their faces and let you listen to their giggles as they tried it out.

Naturally the two hours we had together came and went quickly. It felt like about fifteen minutes. At the end of our time, we were able to sit down and read through some of their records. (Don't Miss This!) The book showed records of when they received their first toothbrush and when they were given shoes. We read about their first goals they had set to simply brush their teeth every day. These were things that are everyday, common sense to me, yet aspects that they had never been taught.

As I walked away that day I realized so much. I realized how much I take for granted every day of my life. I realized how blessed I am. But, most of all, I realized that I am changing those two young girls' stories. One day, they will be sharing with someone else about how they grew up and the story they share will involve this strange, old, bald, white guy from America. I consider it an honor to be a part of their stories.

The truth is, had it not been for people in my life like my parents, friends and Sunday School teachers, I wouldn't have the same story today.

Neither would you.

You Have A Story Too...

Regardless of who you are and no matter where you come from, you have a story. My story entails growing up in a strong Christian home in the middle of Indiana. My dad was an elder in the church where I grew up. I can remember him sometimes preaching for the pastor when he was on vacation. You know that family that's always at church every time the doors are unlocked? That was my family. However, I wouldn't trade it for anything.

When I graduated high school, I was ready to get out of the house and be on my own. I felt called by God to become a pastor so I attended Ozark Christian College in Joplin, Missouri. I loved that school. The professors and friends I had throughout those years will always be part of my story. After two years, though, I questioned whether full-time vocational ministry was right for me. So, I joined the Air Force.

Four years in the military will make you grow up fast, that's for sure. My eyes were opened to the world. I had the opportunity to travel to so many places around the globe like Turkey, England, and Italy. While in Italy, I even took a weekend trip to Rome. It's one thing to see pictures of the Coliseum and the Sistine Chapel. It's totally different to see them in real life. Those four years, the places where I traveled, and the friends I made became permanent parts of my story.

I could continue for page after page about my story, but I think you get the point. I have a story and so do you. In fact, if it were not for the people you've had in your life, you would have a completely different story to tell today. Take just a moment and think about it. What has led you to this point in your life? Who has had an influence in your life? I'm confident that if you're a follower of Christ, you've had people who have had a spiritual influence in your life as well. Without them, you probably would not be the person you are today.

That's the power you hold in your hand.

You have the power to be a story-changer!

Be A Story-Changer...

I'm guessing you've probably already changed some stories, whether you realize it or not. However, most people fail to think about it. Sure, we have friends with whom we go out to eat and to the movies. But rarely do we stop to consider the potential we have to change their life story. I wonder if anyone is telling their story today and their story involves you.

There's a story in the Bible about a woman who went to the local well to get some water one day. Her experience that day changed her story. It seems that Jesus had been traveling through her town and was tired. So he took a break at what we know today to be *Jacob's Well*. As she approached the well to get water, Jesus asked her for a drink.

If that's all you read of the story, it wouldn't seem too dramatic. You need to understand some history. This lady was a Samaritan woman and Jesus was a Jew. In their day, Samaritans despised the Jews and the Jews despised the Samaritans. They would never talk to each other for any reason whatsoever. (Think of the most intense football rivalry you're familiar with and multiply it times about a hundred!) Furthermore, you need to understand that women in their day were not highly favored. They were not looked upon as human but more as a commodity. To say that it was uncommon for a male Jew to speak to a female Samaritan would be an understatement.

After a brief dialogue, Jesus instructed the woman to go and get her husband to which she informed Jesus that she didn't have a husband. Check out Jesus' response...

> *Jesus said, "You're right! You don't have a husband— 18 for you have had five husbands, and you aren't even married to the man you're living with now. You certainly spoke the truth!"* (John 4:17-18)

The woman was amazed because she hadn't shared with Jesus any of those details. Through the rest of the story, she realizes that she is in the presence of a very special person. She drops everything and runs back into town, and can you guess what she does? She begins to share with everyone her story.

Her story had been dramatically changed.

When your story is dramatically changed, you have to tell others.

In verse 39 of that same chapter we read that "many Samaritans" began to believe all because one man touched the life of one woman who then shared her story.

Later, in John chapter 11, one of Jesus' best friends dies. His name was Lazarus. Here's the odd thing in this story. Jesus had actually been informed that Lazarus was sick a couple days before he died. Let me ask you something. If you know you have the ability to heal people and you find out that your best friend is deathly ill, wouldn't you rush to your friend's rescue? I would! Yet, we read that Jesus remained where he was for two days after he had received the news.

Jesus finally decides to head his way and when he arrives he finds out that Lazarus had actually been dead now for four days. Lazarus' sisters begin to rebuke Jesus for not being there in their time of need. There are a lot of details in the story, but at the end of the day, Jesus raises Lazarus from the dead. And here's what we read…

> *Many of the people who were with Mary believed in Jesus when they saw this happen.* (John 8:45)

Because of this one man's influence, stories changed.
    The people who saw what Jesus did were touched.
    Mary and Martha were influenced.
    Lazarus' story definitely changed!
    I realize that we're talking about Jesus, but I want you to know that you have the ability to change stories too! In fact, as a Christian, you are commanded to do so.

The Great Suggestion…

Here's what I see so often. I'm no stranger to this myself either. Our lives end up getting filled with so much busyness that more often than not we miss those opportunities to touch someone's life and change their story. Then we shrug it off. We say, it is what it is. It's just a missed opportunity. Somebody else will come along and seize that opportunity. But I'm not going to lose any sleep over it.

One lady at Christ's Church posted a comment on social media one day that caught my eye and my heart. She wrote this...

> Sometimes I think when I go to church on Sunday, instead of asking myself "how many people are here that I invited" - I should bow my head & apologize to God for those that (even unknowingly) I may have turned away from coming. (Anonymous)

I wish I had that perspective more often. She totally gets the effect of a missed opportunity to change someone's story.

Matthew records the words of Jesus in his gospel account in chapter 28. If you've been in the church for any length of time then you've probably heard this called *The Great Commission*.

> 18 Then Jesus came to them and said, "All authority in heaven and on earth has been given to me. 19 Therefore go and make disciples of all nations, baptizing them in the name of the Father and of the Son and of the Holy Spirit, 20 and teaching them to obey everything I have commanded you. And surely I am with you always, to the very end of the age." (Matt. 28:18-20)

In our day and age, most followers of Christ have not truly taken those words upon themselves as a command. They don't view the words of Christ as a mandate to seize every opportunity. Rather, we view these words as more of a suggestion. But here's the reality, the Great Commission is not just a great suggestion!

The Great Commission is not just a great SUGGESTION!

It's not just a suggestion.
It's not just a good idea.
It's not just words of wisdom.

The word *therefore* in verse 19 may seem insignificant, but it's very important. That one simple little word attaches what is to follow to what was just stated.

In other words, Jesus is saying that there is no one in heaven nor on earth who has more authority than himself. This isn't like your boss at work. This isn't the same as your captain in the military. This is your Commander In Chief - the top dog. No one has more authority. No one ever has nor ever will.

So, here are your orders. Being a follower of Christ is not just about going to church on Sunday. It's not just about being in a small group. It's not just about tossing some money in the offering basket or singing some songs. From the very words of Jesus Christ himself, if you are going to be His follower, you are commanded to *make disciples*! You are commanded to seize every opportunity to share and show Jesus to others! To change stories. Because the One with complete authority is issuing those orders, you now have complete authority to carry them out. When you have that kind of authority which has come from the one who holds ALL authority, you should begin to feel a giant swell of confidence within you!

His Authority Leads To Confidence...

It's interesting to me that the English word *authority* is derived from the Latin word *auctoritas*. That Latin word is the same word used for our English word *invention*. Take Apple, for example, the one who invented the iPod. When I was growing up we had cassette tapes. Remember those? Before that was the record. There was the 8-track tape at one point. After cassettes came compact discs. Then Apple came along and created a way to carry around 1,000 songs in your hip pocket. They are one of the leading authorities when it comes to technology like that. Other companies have gained ground, but I'm guessing you either have an Apple product, use iTunes, or at a minimum, you have at least been affected in some way by the inventor. If it's up to me and I want to know about media portability, I would go straight to the inventor.

So, Jesus is saying to his disciples, *look guys, look around. You see all this? See the trees? See the mountains? See the animals? Yeah, I made all that. I AM the authority. And because I AM the authority, because I AM the one in charge around here, here are my orders for you. Because I AM the authority, you should have full confidence as you follow these orders.*

In fact, the entire Gospel of Matthew stresses the authority of Jesus Christ. For example...

> *...for he taught with real authority—quite unlike their teachers of religious law.* (Matt. 7:29)

> *So I will prove to you that the Son of Man has the authority on earth to forgive sins." Then Jesus turned to the paralyzed man and said, "Stand up, pick up your mat, and go home!"* (Matt. 9:6)

> *Jesus called his twelve disciples together and gave them authority to cast out evil spirits and to heal every kind of disease and illness.* (Matt. 10:1)

Then, at the close of his gospel, Matthew makes it crystal clear that Jesus has ALL authority and with that authority Jesus instructs us to *make disciples.*

There's a difference, though, found in how Jesus handled authority and how the majority of folks in our culture today handle authority. When I think of authority figures in our culture today, naturally, I think of the role of the President and the government around him. I think of police officers and the authority they have been given. I think of a training instructor at a military boot camp. I think of a CEO and the authority he or she may exercise overseeing the company. I'm guessing you've probably seen what I've seen. How often have you seen authority go straight to the person's head? Straight to their ego? Ever met someone like that? Someone you know if given too much authority then we won't be able to fit his fat head through the doorway? I see it everyday.

Jesus' desire in stating his authority wasn't to brag. He wasn't trying to flaunt his authority over others. It wasn't even to establish control and pull rank. Rather, the sole reason that Jesus reminds his disciples of his authority was simply to reassure them.

I can remember when my daughter was younger, we rented a house with a pool in the back yard. My daughter is a water freak. Like many kids, she loves to swim. However, in the beginning, I couldn't get her to jump in the pool. I could stand in the shallow end with water only up to my waist, arms stretched up high, reassuring her that I'd catch her. However, she couldn't see my strong arms. All she could see was the danger of the pool. What do you say in that moment? If you're like me, your urge might be to cluck like a chicken and make fun of her. Thankfully my fatherly instinct kicked in before I opened my mouth. You wouldn't tell your child that you *might* catch her. You wouldn't say, *I'll catch you if I feel like it*. Rather, you reassure your child and that reassurance establishes the confidence to act.

Are you catching my point yet? When Jesus, who has all authority in heaven and on earth, reassures you, it no longer matters what others think nor say about you. It doesn't matter how deep the pool is. It doesn't matter how dangerous the water may be because your Father will catch you!

Jesus is saying, before I continue my thought, before I share what's coming after the "therefore," let me just reassure you of my authority. Not to brag. But, just in case you've forgotten. Just in case you may be questioning things. Just in case you may have shifted your focus off of me and onto this world. Let me remind you that there is nothing on earth nor in hell that has ever been able to hold me down! There is no power and no other authority higher than mine in heaven nor on earth.

I AM the Great I AM!!!

Now go change some stories!

His Mandate Should Be Your Lifestyle...

I shared earlier about how easy it is to lose the meaning of a bible passage in translation. In our modern-day church, we have convinced ourselves that to GO is the command. I don't know how many times I've said that before. That's what I've always thought. However, in the original Greek, Jesus didn't command his disciples to GO. I know it reads like that in our English language. When you read, "therefore, go into all the world," it reads like a command. It reads as though it's something you can just schedule on your calendar. We'll GO next week. We'll GO into the community Sunday afternoon. We'll GO on a mission trip next Summer. Jesus says GO so let's plan to GO. All of that is good and valuable. In no way is my goal to diminish all of the good works Christians have done and continue to do around the globe. But when you read, "Therefore, go into all the world," in the original Greek, it's not a command. It's actually a present participle (my grammar teacher would be so proud that I still know what that means!). In other words, this isn't something you are to plan. It's not something you schedule. It's not a mission trip. It's a lifestyle!

GOing is the way you are to live.

GOing is what you should be doing all day long.

You don't *plan* to go, you *live* to go!

When you go back and read the original Greek, the only command in this passage is when Jesus says *make disciples*. In other words, while you are going, make disciples. Because you are always going to be going, why not go ahead and make some disciples. Because going is your lifestyle, let's make disciples of all the nations. Then Jesus follows that command with *how* to make disciples - teach them to obey and baptize them.

I believe this is one of the main reasons that the American church has been filled with more consumers than contributors. For example, it's easy to get into the mindset that if I put money in the offering plate, that should go to pay the salaries of all the pastors so that they can go and do all the ministry. That's the mentality for many in the local church today. As a result, the church is full of a bunch of spectators watching the game from the stands. If you're a follower of Christ, however, you have been called to get in the game.

You have been called to go.
You have been called to change stories.

But in your hearts revere Christ as Lord. Always be prepared to give an answer to everyone who asks you to give the reason for the hope that you have. (1 Pet. 3:15)

Are you ready? Are you ready to change stories? The simple fact is that you would not have the story you have, had it not been for the influential people you've had throughout your life. I'm confident that as you make *going* your lifestyle, you'll begin to see each and every moment throughout the day as a unique opportunity.

So, go invite a friend to church.
Go sponsor a Compassion child.
Go and reach out to your neighbors who are lost.
Go and be a story-changer!

NOTE: *If you'd like more information about how to rescue a child from poverty, visit www.compassion.com.*

CHAPTER 7

Defeating The Drift:
Overcoming Hurt, Pain & Loss
Part 1

When I was in the seventh grade I lost my Dad. It was 8:30am and he was a block away from work when a car swerved across the center yellow line and hit him head on. He had his seat belt on, but this was long before the age of airbags. This was also long before the age of plastic sunglasses. As the car hit him head on, his head slammed into the steering wheel shattering the glass sunglasses around his eyes and forehead. The roof of the car buckled downward on top of him. I'm not sure if he had clean underwear on, but I'm fairly certain they weren't afterwards.

He was rushed to the local county hospital where we lived in Indiana. I will never forget the moment when I was called out of class at school to find my grandparents and my sister waiting. Uncertainty like that will crush even the strongest person.

The doctors ran some tests to find that his skull had been fractured and they didn't expect him to live. They didn't have the medical equipment needed to care for him so they decided to transfer him to Park View Hospital in Fort Wayne, Indiana.

Fort Wayne was about a 2-hour ambulance ride away. Throughout those two hours, we literally had people from every area of the state praying for my Dad. What happened next was a miracle.

Doctors are smart. I know they're human and they make mistakes just like the rest of us. But, they don't often make huge mistakes. That's why I honestly believe God performed a miracle on my dad throughout that 2-hour ambulance ride. After arriving at Park View, the doctors there ran more tests and found the previous ones to be incorrect. Come to find out, my dad did not have a fracture to his skull. Rather, he had a severe concussion and would be just fine.

So, you didn't really lose your dad that day, huh?

For the past thirty years, my dad has suffered from what Dr. Diamond from the Diamond Headache Clinic in Chicago, Illinois calls *Severe Migraine Headaches*. Yes, my dad lived. But, in light of the fact that just the day before we were playing catch with a baseball in the back yard, and now those times are gone, it felt like I lost my dad. For the rest of my teenage years growing up at home, I saw my dad spend the majority of his time on a couch, in a dark room, with an ice pack on his head. He had to file for disability because he couldn't work. My Mom became the breadwinner in our family. And my family would never be the same.

Imagine the last headache you had. Now multiply that pain, stress and anxiety by about ten. Are you irritable when you have a headache like that? I am. I'm not a very nice person. That kind of pain is what my dad endures nearly twenty-four hours per day... Everyday!

What do you do with that kind of hurt?

How is my father supposed to deal with being let down on his hopes and dreams in life? How is my mother supposed to manage the household while working more than full time? How are my sister and I supposed to deal with a physically-present father who's in constant pain?

The hurt was huge. The pain was unbearable. The loss wasn't fair.

I'm guessing you've been hurt before.

Unattended Pain Will Govern Your Actions...

Unless you live under a rock, I'm sure you remember the whole *Angry Birds* craze from several years ago. Everyone went crazy downloading the free game on their smartphones and notepads and we all got addicted to helping the birds regain their precious eggs. That's the gist of the game. There are these ugly green pigs who steal the birds' eggs. Then the birds use a catapult to launch themselves at the pigs attempting to get back their eggs. They sacrifice themselves seeking revenge, which is another topic for another day. It was a puzzle game and once you completed one level you would move on to the next.

Christ's Church created a message series based on the game and it was one of the most hard-hitting series we had ever done. Not because of the angry birds, but because of how we learned to deal with the hurt, pain and loss when the ugly green pigs in our lives steal what is most important to us.

One of the very first lessons we learned was that *unattended pain will govern your actions.* In other words, if you are hurt, if someone makes you mad, if you are stabbed in the back, if you lose a loved one or find out a loved one is extremely sick - it doesn't matter what the situation - when you have unattended hurt, pain or loss in your life, your actions will emerge out of that hurt, pain or loss. What you say, how you think, and how you react will be influenced by that internal pain. It's the entire concept of the game *Angry Birds*. The nasty green pigs have stolen the birds' eggs and now the birds are retaliating.

Is that your response when someone hurts you... to retaliate?

Our culture is formed around revenge. You hit me and I'm gonna hit you back, twice! The question is this. How would God prefer for you to respond? I want to look at the life of Job in the Bible to answer that question. Job had everything. He lost everything. So how did he survive?

How Much Did He Really Lose?
Job was one of the wealthiest individuals of his day known to mankind. He had it all. In their day, wealth was not measured by one's bank account or the stock market. Wealth was not measured by money, but rather by assets. I thought it would be wise to list out a few things here so we could truly see how wealthy Job was and just how much he lost.

- Job owned 7,000 sheep. One sheep cost around $45, multiplied by 7,000 = $315,000 worth of sheep. (That's a bunch of lamb chops.)
- Job owned 3,000 camels. One camel cost about $125, multiplied by 3,000 = $375,000 worth of camels.
- Job owned 500 yokes of oxen would which would equate to at least 1,000 oxen because it takes at least 2 oxen (plural of ox) to form a yoke. Could have been more. One ox cost around $4,000, multiplied by 1,000 = $4,000,000 worth of oxen.
- Job owned 500 donkeys. One donkey costs about $1,200, multiplied by 500 = $600,000.

Add all of that up and we find that Job was worth more than $5.29 million dollars. In his day, Job was Bill Gates. The Bible describes him as "The greatest of all the people of the east." However, more than $5.29 million dollars is taken away. Here's what happens.

> *In the land of Uz there lived a man whose name was Job. This man was blameless and upright; he feared God and shunned evil. 2 He had seven sons and three daughters, 3 and he owned seven thousand sheep, three thousand camels, five hundred yoke of oxen and five hundred donkeys, and had a large number of servants. He was the greatest man among all the people of the East.* (Job 1:1-3)

> *One day the angels came to present themselves before the LORD, and Satan[b] also came with them. 7 The LORD said to Satan, "Where have you come from?" Satan answered the LORD, "From roaming throughout the earth, going back and forth on it." 8 Then the LORD said to Satan, "Have you considered my servant Job? There is no one on earth like him; he is blameless and upright, a man who fears God and shuns evil." 9 "Does Job fear God for nothing?" Satan replied. 10 "Have you not put a hedge around him and his household and everything he has? You have blessed the work of his hands, so that his flocks and herds are spread throughout the land.* (Job 1:6-10)

In other words, Satan is saying, *Well, of course Job believes in you. Of course Job has faith in you. Look at what you have done for him. Look at how you have blessed him.*

Have you ever met someone like that? Someone, where it seems like everything the person touches turns to gold. They get blessing after blessing after blessing. They're never dealt a poor hand of cards. They always get the Ace of Spades. Their stocks were the ones that didn't crash. Their children are always perfect. They have a perfect marriage. The perfect job. Of course they think life is grand. Of course they love God with all their hearts. That's easy when they have everything they've ever wished for. Have you ever met someone like that? I just wanna smack 'em!

So, Satan presents a little challenge to God. Check it out...

But now stretch out your hand and strike everything he has, and he will surely curse you to your face. (Job 1:11)

God allows this to happen. Note that God does not *cause* this. Satan is the one who *caused* all of the destruction we're about to read. But, God did allow it. Here's what happens in Job's first test...

One day when Job's sons and daughters were feasting and drinking wine at the oldest brother's house, 14 a messenger came to Job and said, "The oxen were plowing and the donkeys were grazing nearby, 15 and the Sabeans attacked and made off with them. They put the servants to the sword, and I am the only one who has escaped to tell you!" 16 While he was still speaking, another messenger came and said, "The fire of God fell from the heavens and burned up the sheep and the servants, and I am the only one who has escaped to tell you!" 17 While he was still speaking, another messenger came and said, "The Chaldeans formed three raiding parties and swept down on your camels and made off with them. They put the servants to the sword, and I am the only one who has escaped to tell you!" 18 While he was still speaking, yet another messenger came and said, "Your sons and daughters were feasting and drinking wine at the oldest brother's house, 19 when suddenly a mighty wind swept in from the desert and struck the four corners of the house. It collapsed on them and they are dead, and I am the only one who has escaped to tell you!" (Job 1:13-19)

I cannot begin to imagine the hurt, pain and loss that Job is now experiencing. I only have one daughter and if I lost her, I don't think

I'd be able to face another day. Job loses everything. But, look at how he responds...

> At this, Job got up and tore his robe and shaved his head. Then he fell to the ground in worship. (Job 1:20)

Your Opportunity To Worship...

What's your first natural instinct when something negative happens? How do you react? Most would have to admit that their reaction is probably not the ideal. Job worships. I'm guessing that's not what you want to hear. Cause, I'll be honest, when I've been hurt, or stabbed in the back, or I've experienced loss of some sort, worshipping God is not exactly the first thing I think of doing.

Job didn't go off the deep end. He didn't start pointing the finger at others. He didn't start casting blame. He didn't even go off on God. He simply worshipped. And he didn't stop there. Check out what he actually said while worshipping...

> "Naked I came from my mother's womb, and naked I will depart. The LORD gave and the LORD has taken away; may the name of the LORD be praised." (Job 1:21)

He doesn't leave his pain alone so that his pain alone may govern his actions. He acknowledged that nothing in this life was ever his to begin with. I think a lot of times, the hurt that we experience stems from the ownership we have created within our own hearts. In other words, I get so attached to my daughter. She is my girl, right!? She would have never been born had it not been for my wife and me. If she were taken away, if she suddenly came down with some sort of disease, I don't know that worshipping God would necessarily be my first action. My perspective of ownership begins to dictate how I treat that situation. That hurt begins to govern my actions.

What is your perspective? How do you view your *things*? Is your car yours or is it a blessing that God has given to you? Is your job yours or is it a blessing that God has given to you to make a living? You see, more often than not we grasp ahold of those things in our lives with a death grip on them because we are afraid of losing them. And when we lose those things we fear we'll also lose control, but here's the reality, when you fear God there's nothing else to fear!

**When you fear God
there's nothing else to fear!**

When you hold a healthy fear of God then there is nothing that could ever happen to you, or be said about you, that will shake you. What's your first response when life goes down the tubes?

Your Opportunity To Influence Others...
The story goes on and the pain doesn't end for Job. In chapter 2, he loses even more. In the first test, we find that God prevented Satan from inflicting any kind of physical harm upon Job. In this second test, though, Satan presses God even further. And here's what happens to Job...

> 7 So Satan went out from the presence of the LORD and afflicted Job with painful sores from the soles of his feet to the crown of his head. 8 Then Job took a piece of broken pottery

> and scraped himself with it as he sat among the ashes. 9 His wife said to him, "Are you still maintaining your integrity? Curse God and die!" 10 He replied, "You are talking like a foolish woman. Shall we accept good from God, and not trouble?" In all this, Job did not sin in what he said. (Job 2:7-8)

Worshipping God is not exactly our first response to pain nor do we typically view it as an opportunity to influence others. When I'm hurting, that is my time to wallow in my own grief, right? I mean, this is the time for others to take care of me. This is the time for me to have my self-pity party and for others to help me nurse that pain. However, if you can take care of that pain without allowing it to take care of you, you just may have the opportunity to influence others who are around you.

It's difficult for someone like me to see the kind of pain that my father has endured for decades. You can't see when someone has a headache. You might notice a little something on their face, but, it's not like they're bleeding. You can't see broken bones or sores.

I can remember asking him one time just how bad the pain was. This was his response: *"Have you ever been in so much pain that you just wish you were dead?"*

Maybe you can relate to that kind of hurt and loss.

Regardless, in over 30 years of pain, I have watched my dad seize opportunity after opportunity. He has literally influenced thousands of lives. I'm confident he has no clue just how many people he has touched. All while enduring incredible amounts of pain.

We find Job in severe physical pain. From head to toe. Imagine the most pain that you have endured throughout your lifetime. Isn't it true that when you are in that much pain, *you* are easily influenced? From the life of Job we realize that whom you surround yourself with will either influence you or you will influence them!

**Whom you surround yourself with will either influence you...
Or you will influence them!**

In other words, those you surround yourself with will either bring your spirit down or lift your spirit up. You'll do the same for them.

Asking "Why" Causes More Pain...

In the following chapter of Job, he begins to ask the same question you and I have asked probably hundreds of times. *Why?*

> *"Why is light given to those in misery, and life to the bitter of soul, 21 to those who long for death that does not come, who search for it more than for hidden treasure, 22 who are filled with gladness and rejoice when they reach the grave?* (Job 3:20-22)

In the final verse of Chapter 3, we find exactly what happens to all of us when we persist in wrestling with the *why* question..

> *I have no peace, no quietness; I have no rest, but only turmoil.* (Job 3:26)

Now, don't get me wrong, there's no sin in asking why. It's not wrong to ask why. You're not offending God or breaking his heart by asking why. I am right there with most of you who's first natural instinct is to ask why.

Listen!
Don't miss this next point!

It's the manner in which we ask *why* that will get us in trouble!

It's actually a healthy thing to ask God *why*. In order for you to ask God you have to get close to God. I think God likes it when you draw close to him. Rather than avoiding Him all together, you are actually approaching God. That's a very good thing as long as you do not sin in the approach.

Our struggle is actually found in the fact that God's ways are higher than your ways. You're just wasting your time to try and understand what God is doing.

> *Trust in the LORD with all your heart and lean not on your own understanding; 6 in all your ways submit to him, and he will make your paths straight.* (Prov. 3:5-6)

That does not say God will give you everything you want. It says God will show you direction. It doesn't even say that God's going to give you a GPS unit and show you the final destination. You see, when the Bible says to *lean not on your own understanding*, what that tells us is that no matter how often we ask *why*, we'll probably never get the answer this side of heaven. And if you do get the answer you probably won't understand it. It's beyond your capacity to comprehend. It's beyond your ability to see the big picture. Which, if you're like me, only causes more frustration... more confusion... and more pain.

When you study the life of Job you'll never discover *why* you suffer.

You'll discover *how* to suffer.

How you suffer will dramatically impact whether you drift in this life.

CHAPTER 8

Defeating The Drift: Overcoming Hurt, Pain & Loss Part 2

It's not about why we suffer.
It's about *how* we suffer.
There's another paradigm shift for you. That one single change in your outlook on life could very well change your entire opinion when it comes to suffering. All of a sudden the concern is no longer about losing $5.29 million dollars worth of possessions. The focus is on how you react when you do. Simple physics states that *a constant force will cause a constant change*. The question, then, is which direction will that change take you.

When you experience any kind of hurt, pain, or loss, if you want to have any kind of hope that you will successfully come out of that situation, then there are conditions attached to that hope.

—⚘—

Hope always comes with conditions attached to it.

—⚘—

Too often, however, we view this aspect of hope in our lives as a noun rather than a verb. Hope is something you *do* not just something you *have!* For example, if you're having struggles in your marriage, it's easy to give up hope. If you are going to have any hope to regain marital momentum, you're gonna have to take some action steps!

If you hope to move up the corporate ladder in your workplace, then you should know that you cannot merely sit around and do nothing while you're on the clock. You have to work at it. You have to put in some extra effort. Show your employer that you can take the initiative.

If you hope to make the football team in the fall and you sit around eating Twinkies all day long and get out of shape, when it comes time for try outs, you won't keep up with everyone else. (I know. I eat a lot of Twinkies!)

Hope always comes with conditions attached to it. You cannot hope for something and then not take steps towards seeing that hope become a reality. More often than not, what we hope for is within our means so long as we are able to recognize those conditions and then begin to strive after them.

In light of what we spoke about in the previous chapter, if we have unattended hurt, pain, or loss in our lives, it will quickly turn our hope from a verb into a noun. Our hope will quickly be paralyzed. And we will quickly find ourselves doing absolutely nothing to see that hope become a reality. Why? Because unattended pain will govern your actions.

We've spoken about Job and everything that he lost. Next, three friends of his come to try and explain what's going on. I don't want to dwell on them too long. But, I will point out that their own personal experiences in life were the foundation for their explanation. They tried to compare their experiences with Job. They had a one-upping contest to see whose hurt and pain was worse. And ultimately they belittled Job. Their basic perspective in life was *do what is right and things will go well for you... do what is wrong and you'll be punished for it.* So, Job, you've lost everything. Therefore, you must have done some really horrible things. Job, your children have been killed because either they are sinners, you are a sinner, or maybe both. Time to come clean, bro. Time to fess up. Obviously, they had no clue what they were talking about.

Neither do we when we are faced with hurt like that.

Better to be silent than say anything at all.

You've learned that, right?

Grounded In The Character Of God...

So, everything has been taken away from Job. He's enduring immense physical pain. Even his own wife wishes that he would just die. Things aren't looking too good for Job. His three friends try to explain things to him with a theology that's way out in left field. The first two have spoken and now the third, named *Zophar*, speaks. (Please don't name your boy that. Sounds like someone out of a hokey sci-fi movie!)

> *Oh, how I wish that God would speak, that he would open his lips against you 6 and disclose to you the secrets of wisdom, for true wisdom has two sides. Know this: God has even forgotten some of your sin. 7 "Can you fathom the mysteries of God? Can you probe the limits of the Almighty?* (Job 11:5-7)

Wisdom has two sides. In other words, there's the small, little, tiny, itty-bitty speck that we see. Then there's what God sees. The fact is this, you and I will never, this side of heaven, have the ability to comprehend the wisdom of God. Therefore, our source for hope has to begin with the character of God.

If you could set aside the magnitude of what has just happened to Job, no matter how horrible the situation was, he didn't have the same insight that we have today. Job didn't have the Bible. Job didn't know the end of the story like we do. Job didn't have any of the New Testament scriptures, which reveal so much about the character of God to us today.

For example, in the presence of your misery, God is compassionate. In the presence of your guilt, God offers grace. In the presence of your sin, God hands you mercy. In the presence of your confession, God freely gives you his unconditional love. After all, that's why he sent his one and only son to die on a cross in the first place. So that amidst your hurt, pain and loss you can still have hope.

Job didn't have that scriptural insight.

Do you understand how good we have it?

Back in the day of the Israelites, you couldn't go straight to God. If you tried to pray to God back then, it'd be the same as going to a giant oak tree in the back yard. The only way to go to God back then was through the *High Priest*. And then the high priest went to God for you. They had this place called the *Holy of Holies* where the presence of God existed. Only the High Priest was allowed in the Holy of Holies. As a matter of fact, anyone other than the High Priest who entered into the Holy of Holies would die. (I know, it was some real Indiana Jones stuff!) On top of that, even the High Priest was only allowed into this place once a year. That doesn't seem like a very personal God to me! That doesn't sound like a God who's compassionate and graceful and merciful and loving.

Today, it's totally different. Now that Jesus has come and has been offered as a sacrifice for you and me, you have the privilege to go straight to God. Check this out...

> *Therefore, since we have a great high priest who has ascended into heaven, Jesus the Son of God, let us hold firmly to the faith we profess. 15 For we do not have a high priest*

> who is unable to empathize with our weaknesses, but we have one who has been tempted in every way, just as we are—yet he did not sin. 16 Let us then approach God's throne of grace with confidence, so that we may receive mercy and find grace to help us in our time of need. (Heb. 4:14-16)

Doesn't that sound better? That sounds like a very personal God. And those personal characteristics of God are exactly where you can begin to find hope throughout times of hurt, pain, and loss. In light of the fact that hope always comes with conditions attached to it, it's still YOUR choice whether you will look for that hope in the character of God.

The Unbreakable Confidence In God...

So, now we have heard from all three of Job's friends. Each has taken his turn making a fool of himself, trying to explain to Job why things happen as they do. Job then begins to plead his case. I love where he begins...

> What you know, I also know; I am not inferior to you. 4 You, however, smear me with lies; you are worthless physicians, all of you! 5 If only you would be altogether silent For you, that would be wisdom. (Job 13:2; 4-5)

In other words, shut it down! Just stop talking. Job is disappointed. But he's not expressing disappointment in his loss. He's not expressing disappointment in his circumstances. He's disappointed in his friends. I truly believe Job's friends wanted to help him, but not at the sake of their own reputations. They continued to see only the surface of what was happening, and they refused to look deeper. As a result, they provided much more harm than they did help.

Ever had a friend like that? Friends who are more concerned about themselves than they are you and your problems? They come to your aid but that aid feels more like an obligation they are trying to fulfill.

It happens in the church all the time. I believe it's one of the main reasons so many have fallen away from the church. We all have presumptions about what we're supposed to experience in church, the character of the people, and how we're supposed to be treated. Yet I would venture to say that in the majority of churches, people act the part because they are *expected* to act the part, not because they want to.

Disappointment in your friends will crush your spirit. So will uncertainty. That's the next direction Job goes...

> *"Keep silent and let me speak; then let come to me what may. 14 Why do I put myself in jeopardy and take my life in my hands? 15 Though he slay me, yet will I hope in him; I will surely defend my ways to his face. 16 Indeed, this will turn out for my deliverance, for no godless person would dare come before him! 17 Listen carefully to what I say; let my words ring in your ears.* (Job 13:13-17)

I tried quoting the first part of verse 13 to my wife once. It didn't pan out too well! Seriously, I believe this passage to be one of the greatest declarations of faith found anywhere in the Bible. Job is placing his life in the hands of God. Even though God *allowed* Satan to take everything away from Job, he still places his life in the hands of God.

Where do you turn when life seems uncertain?

Where do you turn when you have questions?

Where do you turn when your life is filled with all kinds of *what ifs*?

Job turned to the living God!

We have all kinds of uncertainty in our day and age. Uncertain about job security. Uncertain whether your spouse will still be there when you wake up in the morning. Uncertain about whether there will be enough money to get through till the next payday. Uncertain about your health. Uncertain about whether your car is gonna keep running. The list goes on and on. Where do we turn for answers?

Maybe you turn to family. Or, like Job, maybe your friends begin to step up. Sometimes we turn to therapists. None of those people are harmful, but rather than turning to the positive, many people turn to negative and harmful coping mechanisms.

Drugs, hoping they will deaden the uncertainties.

Violence, hoping to conquer their uncertainties.

Alcohol, hoping to ignore their uncertainties.

Even suicide, hoping to escape from their uncertainties.

These are very real emotions that cause very real actions. Rather than hoping and healing, we run and hide.

I'm guessing there are probably some of you, though, who are probably thinking that you'd never go to those extremes. Unfortunately, we still adopt all kinds of unhealthy habits. For example, emotional eating. Compulsive spending. Over sleeping. Under sleeping. Hitting walls. (C'mon, you know you've done that!) For me, I go home and kill terrorists on my Playstation. That's how I cope.

Some people just ignore everything.

Why is it that we rarely turn to God? Why isn't our first response not to pray or read our Bible? Even rarer do we make a claim as Job did, *Though he slay me, yet will I hope in him.* Here's the hope that we have which answers every uncertainty you may ever face...

Praise be to the God and Father of our Lord Jesus Christ! In his great mercy he has given us new birth into a living hope through the resurrection of Jesus Christ from the dead. (1 Pet. 1:3)

But even that *living hope* comes with the condition that you have to CHOOSE that new birth. Hope always comes with conditions attached to it. That means that you have to begin to place your disappointment, your uncertainty, and even the times you've been betrayed into the hands of God.

I bet no matter who you are, you know what it feels like to be betrayed.

I do.

Job did.

This is when it really gets tough. I wish I were able to butter this up and make it feel better. But that wouldn't be the full truth. Certainly we know that God had not betrayed Job. (Remember, we know the end of the story unlike Job.) Betrayed is exactly how Job felt, though.

Have you ever felt like God has completely turned His back on you? You cry out to God but you hear no answer. It only takes one time feeling betrayed by God Almighty and many folks never give God a second chance. However, here's the difference between how Job handled his situation and how we typically handle ours. Job prepared his case and then went TO God. Look at this...

> *Now that I have prepared my case, I know I will be vindicated.* (Job 13:18)

Say what?

The boy is gonna start a debate with the Man upstairs?

Has he lost his ever-picking mind?

Here's the difference between Job and how we typically respond. Don't miss this! When we feel betrayed, our instinct is to run away from God. We give up on God. We curse God. We blame God. All because we feel like we've been betrayed.

We come full circle back around to the character of God. Because here's what we always forget... or even sometimes choose to ignore. As I mentioned earlier, there are 2 sides to wisdom.

Hope always comes with conditions attached to it. Have you lost all hope and long to be hopeful again? Seek it! It won't just appear. It won't just pop into your heart. It won't just be manifested out of thin air in your life. You have to be grounded in the character and the confidence of God.

> *May the God of hope fill you with all joy and peace as you trust in him, so that you may overflow with hope by the power of the Holy Spirit.* (Rom. 15:13)

Do you see the condition?

You get hope... as a matter of fact, you will *overflow* with hope. But, first it requires you to *trust* God.

What About When I'm In The Friends' Shoes?

Let's reverse the roles and talk about when you're not the one struggling, but you have a friend who is. What do you do? What do you say? As a general rule of thumb, it's better to say nothing at all than it is to open your mouth and cause more pain. That's exactly what Job's three friends did. They thought they had all the answers. But as they spoke they only made things worse.

We are typically scared of silence. I don't know why. It makes us uncomfortable. It creates awkward moments. For some reason we equate silence with something not quite being right. As a result of being uncomfortable with the silence we try to fill in the silence. Oftentimes the outcome is what we would call... sticking your foot in your mouth. Eliphaz, the oldest and "wisest" of Job's friends, pulls a real doozy - sticks his foot right inside of his mouth. Check this out...

> *Your sin prompts your mouth; you adopt the tongue of the crafty.* (Job 15:5)

I don't know about you, but it helps me if I use different voices for the various characters when I'm reading a story in the Bible like this. Eliphaz sounds just like the Church Lady from old-school Saturday Night Live. Go ahead and read it again. If you're in public, go ahead and read it like the Church Lady... out loud!

Let me ask you a question. If you're hurting, how would you respond if someone spoke to you like Eliphaz did to Job? I know one thing. It didn't help. I love Job's response...

> *I have heard many things like these; you are miserable comforters, all of you!* (Job 16:2)

You are miserable comforters. That's funny! Probably wasn't in the moment. I believe Job's friends were missing a critical key component. A component that you an I need in times when our friends are struggling with hurt. You need the Comforter before you can begin to provide the comfort.

This isn't rocket science. I truly believe that by ourselves, the comfort we have to offer others will be limited. It very well may be short-sighted. We may not fully understand the situation the other person is going through. We will be operating out of our own strength rather than through the power of the Holy Spirit in our lives. When we operate through only our strength we will only end up creating more misery.

Do you know the difference between sympathy and empathy? Basically, in its easiest form, sympathy is... *I have no idea what you are feeling but I'm sorry.* Empathy, on the other hand, is... *while I can't understand exactly what you are feeling because every situation is unique, I have had a similar experience so my feelings for you may be more real.* The problem was that Job's friends thought they were offering sympathy and even empathy for Job, when in reality, they offered neither. Paul gives us a great picture of comfort in 2 Corinthians...

> *Praise be to the God and Father of our Lord Jesus Christ, the Father of compassion and the God of all comfort, 4 who comforts us in all our troubles, so that we can comfort those in any trouble with the comfort we ourselves receive from God. 5 For just as we share abundantly in the sufferings of Christ, so also our comfort abounds through Christ. 6 If we are distressed, it is for your comfort and salvation; if we are comforted, it is for your comfort, which produces in you patient endurance of the same sufferings we suffer. 7 And our hope for you is firm, because we know that just as you share in our sufferings, so also you share in our comfort. (2 Cor. 1:3-7)*

In that one little passage that only takes about a minute to read, the word *comfort* is used nine times. It's the Greek word... PARA-KLEE'-SIS. To comfort someone in the New Testament scriptures, it always entailed much more than soothing sympathy. The root word is actually the Latin word... FOR-TEES'... which means, *brave*. In other words, when we have the *Comforter*, meaning the Holy Spirit, now we will find a comfort that brings courage. A comfort that is enabling to those whom we are comforting. A comfort that breathes strength.

Apart from the Holy Spirit, I'm afraid we'll all just be *miserable comforters*. If you've read any of what Eliphaz, Bildad or Zophar have had to say, it doesn't take long to see that their words are full of everything BUT courage, enablement and strength.

I hear all the time about how our culture is more narcissistic than ever. I don't know about you, but I'm seeing some pretty self-centered friends here. Friends who are more concerned about proving to Job that they are right and he is wrong. Friends who are more concerned about their own reputations than they are about the pain Job is enduring.

How do you comfort others?

Do you rely on yourself? Or do you have such a relationship with God that he has given you the *Comforter* enabling you to truly comfort others?

I Pee My Pants Too...

I heard the story one time about a 9-year-old boy. He sat at his desk in school one day when all of a sudden there appeared a puddle between his feet. The front of his pants were wet as well. His heart began to thump harder and harder. He knew when the rest of the boys in the class found out, he'd be the laughing stock of the entire school. When the girls found out, they'd never speak to him again as long as he lives.

The boy put his head down and began to pray... *Dear God, this is an emergency! I need help now! Five minutes from now I'm dead meat.* He looked up from his prayer only to find his teacher approaching him with a look in her eyes that said he'd been discovered. However, as the teacher approached, a classmate named Susie intervened. She carried a goldfish bowl filled with water. She stumbled and dumped the goldfish bowl in his lap.

He pretended to be angry all while praying, *Thank you, Jesus! Thank you, Jesus! Hallelujah, Glory to God. Thank you, Jesus!* Now, rather than being the object of ridicule, this young boy became the object of sympathy. The teacher rushed him downstairs and gave him gym shorts to put on while his pants dried out. When he came back to class, all the kids were on their hands and knees cleaning up around his desk. The sympathy was wonderful!

But as life would have it, the ridicule that should have been his had been transferred to Susie. She tried to help clean things up, but they told her to get out... *You've done enough, you klutz!* As the day progressed, the sympathy for this young boy got better and better, but the ridicule Susie received got worse and worse.

Finally, at the end of the day, they found themselves waiting at the bus stop. The boy walked over to Susie and whispered in her ear... *Susie, you did that on purpose, didn't you?* To which Susie whispered back... *I wet my pants once too.*

What a beautiful picture of empathy.

Seeing Beyond The Current State Of Life...
In chapter 17, Job is ready to die. He's totally ready to give up. He talks about becoming one with the worms. This man is completely broken. Check this out...

> *My spirit is broken, my days are cut short, the grave awaits me. 7 My eyes have grown dim with grief; my whole frame is but a shadow. 11 My days have passed, my plans are shattered. 15 who can see any hope for me?* (Job 17:1,7,11,15)

You see, on the one hand, Job wanted to live long enough to see himself vindicated. He wanted to stay alive long enough so that his three friends, who weren't extremely friendly, would come to the conclusion that Job was right and they were wrong. On the other hand, he didn't know how much more he could endure.

Ever feel like that? Literally, *I don't care... I give up... I don't want to die... but I don't know how much more I can take of this.* Been there? God does not answer Job's plea for death. Can you guess why? Because God had something far better planned for Job!

I believe God has something greater planned for you!

I think we often get confused in our interpretation of exactly what comfort should be or should feel like. Have you ever thought about this? How exactly does God's comfort feel? I think a lot of times we have in our minds that if God truly were to comfort me then he would just take away the pain. He would pick me up out of this situation and place me in a happy place.

However, I think God more often dispenses his comfort in convenient doses like cough medicine. Just enough to keep us going, taking the next step, facing the next day. God doesn't send a "Cure All" for us. He's not going to snap his fingers and magically make all the pain go away like our own personal genie. What God does is something much greater. Rather than giving us some temporary comfort, he sends us the *Comforter*. Oftentimes, when we feel as though we are drowning, we'd rather just swim for the banks.

A couple of years ago a few guys traveled to Zimbabwe to raft the Zambezi River. They boarded their raft at the base of the Victoria Falls where massive amounts of water spill over the top and drop almost a thousand feet. The roar of the falls was deafening to the ears.

Have you seen the Victoria Falls? They are magnificent!

The falls are the largest in the world at more than a mile wide. Mist from the spray that fills the air looks like fog and can be seen from up to fifty miles away. The locals call it *Smoke That Thunders*.

The river holds the world's largest rapids. In the United States, the highest-class rapid you are allowed to raft is a class five. The Zambezi's rapids can top class seven and sometimes an eight.

As the guys sat on the edge of the eight-person raft, all suited up in a tight, overstuffed jacket and a thick crash helmet, the guide began to instruct them. "When the raft flips..." (Wait, wait, wait. Hold on a minute! I'm just gonna be honest with you for a second. If I'm going white-water rafting, I go to get into the raft and the instructor says, "WHEN the raft flips," I'm getting outta the raft!) There was no "If the raft flips." There was no, "On the off chance we get flipped." Nope. It was "*When* the raft flips." He went on, "... stay in the rough water. You will be tempted to swim toward the stagnant water at the edge of the banks. Don't do it. Because it is in the stagnant water that the crocs wait for you." He goes on to say, "They are large and hungry. Even when the raft flips, stay in the rough water."

Have any sympathy for the poor guys?

Not me!

I'll stick to the river raft ride at Dollywood!

But isn't that what we want in life? When we, or our friends, are faced with all kinds of hurt, pain and loss, we begin to make a mad dash towards what appears to be the safety of the stagnant waters. When the raft flips, and it will, what we fail to realize is that what lies beneath the surface is something that will destroy us.

So God says, just go with the flow. Stop running from the chaos and just go through it. You will grow through the pain. You will mature through the hurt.

There's one final, giant aspect that we can't forget. God never sends you the *Comforter* just so you can keep the *Comforter* all to yourself. God sends you the *Comforter* so that you may be comforted, and in turn, know how to comfort others. Again...

> "...the God of all comfort, 4 who comforts us in all our troubles, so that we can comfort those in any trouble with the comfort we ourselves receive from God." (2 Cor. 1:3b-4)

You can defeat the drift through your times of hurt, pain and loss. You can help others defeat the drift as well.

CHAPTER 9

Defeating The Drift: Committing To Worship

You've probably heard the question before. If God is all powerful, is he strong enough to create a rock so large that he, himself, would not be able to move it? Wrong question! However, it does show our human desire to wrap our minds around God and who he is. You probably know by now, that's impossible. If you were to gain that much knowledge about God, your head would probably pop like an overly ripe cherry tomato.

Surprisingly, there is something that God is not powerful enough to provide. In his infinite greatness and unending strength, there is something that he, himself, cannot provide for himself. There is something that he desperately needs and only you can meet that need. Your worship is that one thing that God needs and only you can provide!

—⚎—

Your worship is the one thing that God needs and only you can provide!

—⚎—

God, the Creator of every star, of every planet, of every tree, every blade of grass, every animal, every man and woman, needs you. When God created you and me He decided to create us with free choice. This means that you are not just a puppet on a string or a puppy on a leash. You have the freedom to choose God or leave Him behind. You have the choice to follow Him or to follow the world. Because of God's decision to give us that freedom there is one thing in this universe which he does not have the power to obtain for himself and that is your worship.

In John chapter 4 we find a story about Jesus. He is traveling and comes in contact with a woman. Now, in this time, for a man to speak to a woman who is a stranger was way outside of the box. However, not only did Jesus speak with a female stranger, he was a Jewish male speaking to a Samaritan woman. That's not just outside of the box. That's like a Gator fan speaking with a Bulldog! (Insert your local college rivalry.) You would think that nothing good will come from this. The Jews despised the Samaritans and the Samaritans despised the Jews. So Jesus crosses the line and begins to speak with this woman.

Without knowing this woman personally Jesus begins to speak *about* her. She is in awe of this guy. *How does he know all of this stuff about me?* She realizes that this must be a really holy man and so she asks him a question.

There was this constant debate going on between the Samaritans and the Jews about where to worship. The Samaritans said that you had to go up to the top of a mountain a little ways away. That would get you physically closer to God. The Jews, however, had a different take. They claimed that you are supposed to worship in the temple. That's where the presence of God lives. So, here's this lady and she wants to ask this holy guy where the right place to worship is. And this is how Jesus responds.

> *Yet a time is coming and has now come when the true worshipers will worship the Father in spirit and truth, for they are the kind of worshipers the Father seeks.* (John 4:23)

Couple of observations...

First, if Jesus talks about *true* worshippers then there must be *false* worshippers.

Second, Jesus goes on to say that these *true* worshippers are the kind of people that God *seeks*. That blows my mind! It's completely different from what we've been groomed by our world to seek. Our world seeks the most talented, the most wealthy, the most powerful. Yet, God doesn't care one iota who you are in the world's eyes. What God is looking for is authentic, genuine, real, *true* worshippers. And it's the one thing that God needs that only you can give!

The third observation is this. That verse says *for they are the kind of worshippers the Father seeks.* Is that past, present or future tense? "For they ARE" is present tense. In other words, worship is not something that only happens on Sunday morning. It's not about getting up on Sunday morning, putting on your fine church clothes, walking into a sanctuary, singing a few songs, listening to a message, and then going home. Worship is not something that you do once or twice a week... Worship is what you are!

Worship is what you are!

Here's what I want you to do. The next time someone asks you the generic question, *what do you do,* I want you to respond by telling that person you are a *worshipper*. I bet you'll get some great facial expressions.

What do you do? You're a worshipper. What do you do at work? You worship. What do you do at school? You worship. What do you do at home? You worship. Who are you? You are a worshipper. You have the ability to give God the one thing He desperately wants and cannot obtain for Himself.

Worship In Awe...
In our culture full of idols and altars, I wonder how much awe is even possible to experience when we worship God. In a world that can feed every desire we've ever had, our senses have grown numb to the greatness of God.

I think about *Team Edward* and *Team Jacob* from *Twilight*. Females from every age and background got sucked into the saga. There's nothing wrong with a good movie until that movie begins to shift your awe away from God.

Our world is full of all kinds of people with that kind of impact. From superstar athletes to superstar artists. And as we talk about the person, our awe oozes out of us. I'm afraid to think of what might happen if we were to meet the person in real life. We would go out of our way to make the person comfortable and give him every little thing he needs.

Why don't we give God that kind of awe and attention?

Rather, I hear God being referred to as *The Big Guy* or the *Dude Upstairs*. Maybe you have the T-shirt claiming that *Jesus Is My Homeboy*. I'm sure I probably sound like an old fart, but I feel that God and his Son, Jesus Christ, deserve just a little more awe and respect? True worshippers worship Him with awe! John writes...

In his right hand he held seven stars...His face was like the sun shining in all its brilliance. When I saw him, I fell at his feet as though dead...
(Rev. 1:16-17a)

Sounds to me like Jesus is a little more than just your *homeboy!* The writer of Hebrews says...

Therefore, since we are receiving a kingdom that cannot be shaken, let us be thankful, and so worship God acceptably with reverence and awe, for our God is a consuming fire.
(Heb. 12:28-29)

What exactly does that mean? Our God is a consuming fire? Just a little while ago you told me that God was merciful and loving and graceful. What happened to that?

One of the things we often forget is that God is equally just as he is merciful. If he wanted to, he could snap his fingers and... poof... you'd be gone. Have you realized his power? Actually, I don't think anyone is capable of fully comprehending his power. That's why I am in awe of him.

True worshippers worship God with Awe. Why? Because they are consumed with God. And when you are consumed with God, you will give to God the one thing that He needs and only you can provide - your worship.

Worship With Abandonment...

The thing about famous people is if we have the chance to meet the person, it doesn't matter what anyone else thinks, it doesn't bother you. It doesn't matter who makes fun of you. It doesn't matter how silly it may seem to somebody else. It doesn't bother you, right!? We're not worried about who may see us. We're not worried about who may talk about us behind our back. We don't care because we are totally focussed on that person.

We find a similar instance in the old testament when the Ark of the Covenant was brought into the city of David. King David lost control and worshipped with abandonment. Some may say that he went too far. I wonder what God thought. We find the story in Second Samuel. King David is being criticized by Michal. Look at David's response.

> David said to Michal...'I will celebrate before the LORD. I will become even more undignified than this, and I will be humiliated in my own eyes...'
> (2 Sam. 6:21-22)

Have you ever been at that point?

You find yourself in the presence of the Lord and you let it all pour out? You don't care about who's watching and how crazy they might think you are. And it doesn't matter because you are in the presence of the Almighty God.

The Bible says that David *danced* with all of his might. Let me tell you something. If I stood up and danced with just a little bit of my might (actually if I danced at all) you would laugh! I'm sure you wouldn't hold back. David didn't care because he was in the presence of the Lord.

This wasn't just some ordinary man. He wasn't the neighbor next door. He didn't work in the cubicle next to you. He didn't sit next to you in school. This was the king. This was King David. People looked up to King David. People respected King David. People looked to King David for direction.

I wonder who's watching you.

Do you have kids? They're watching you.

Do you have friends? They're watching you.

I want you to understand that worshipping God with complete awe and abandonment is not just about you and God. There is so much more to the equation. Your worship could actually lead someone else to Christ!

The opposite is true as well, though.

If you do not worship *all out*. If you do not put the pedal to the floor. If you do not worship with complete abandonment. Those who are watching you probably won't either. So, turn that frown upside down! So many people totally overlook this aspect because it's so easy to get internally focussed.

Internally Focussed Worship...

I spent the first twelve years of my ministry in the local church as a worship pastor. Most everybody loves worship... until you don't sing the song they want to sing. Until you sing their favorite song with a twist. Until you sing the same chorus over and over. For years, I found myself right in the middle of the worship wars over which so many churches split. Fortunately, I was never part of a church split, but I sure experienced my fair share of unhappy worshippers.

I had the opportunity to be part of a church plant outside of Atlanta, Georgia. The church began with about thirty-five and had grown to about 150 when I came on board. My task was to develop a praise band. There was just one problem. All I had to work with in the beginning was a pianist and one person playing an old Casio keyboard. (Your phone has better sounds than that thing did!) Nonetheless, I took what was dealt to me and went to work.

Sequencing is a term used by musicians who would automate their music. Back in the day, it was a form of pre-recording your music so that you could have the sound of a full band with a minimum number of musicians throughout the live performance. I sequenced, and I sequenced, and I sequenced. My time each week was consumed with attempting to create a full band sound with only two musicians, but it worked. I had a machine play the guitar, drums, bass, and every other instrument that each song needed.

Did I mention that I had a machine playing the drums? That's right. We had drums in church. Well, we didn't have a real live drum set; just the drum sounds automated from the sequencer. Several months later, though, a drummer stepped up. He was keen enough to know that he heard drums but didn't see anyone playing the drums. (Smart guy!) And he offered to begin playing the drums live.

Get ready. The roller coaster ride is about to begin!

I should also mention that this is a true story. You won't believe how it ends!

I had surrounded myself with some very wise mentors in that church. They advised me rather than using an acoustic drum set to use an electric one. That way our sound guy would have the ability to fully control how prevalent the drums would be in our mix. I fully agreed. I took it one step further, though. Rather than having our drummer begin playing from day one, I merely set the drum set up on stage. Picture this with me. You're in church. You hear a full band including drums. But nobody ever sat down at the drum set for the entire service.

Can you guess what happened?

People began to complain about the drums.

I'm talking irate people!

For the past nine months, they had been hearing the drums in the mix because I programmed them in there. Now, they're actually seeing the drums on stage and they went haywire. It felt like the world had just stopped spinning.

Do you think God was pleased with their worship?

Do you think God continued to *seek* them to meet his need for worship?

They definitely were not abandoned.

Here's what happens. (And I have this temptation just as much as the next person.) Worship becomes all about me rather than all about God. Worship becomes all about what I want. It becomes all about my own preferences and opinions. And if those preferences and opinions are not met, then the problem must be somebody else. After all, my preferences and opinions can't be wrong.

For many, worship has become all about the emotional high that can be achieved. We forget that people are watching us. We forget that people are learning from us how to worship. We forget that those who worship with awe and abandonment will lay everything down at the foot of the cross because there's One who gave all so that you can give your all.

Worship With Intimacy...

Please don't tune out here. If you're a married man, you may be thinking that you don't really need another intimate relationship in your life. I get that. I'm right there with you. But, this is a very important point. Actually, this is one of the most important points in this entire chapter.

First, let me ask you a question. Who is that person you've always dreamed of meeting? Like, you would faint if you stumbled upon the person in the airport. Awe might be a pretty good word to describe your reaction. But, do you really *know* that person? You may know *of* him, but you don't really know that person, right? You may know the person's favorite food. You may know what kind of car the person drives. You may know what the news has reported about the person. You may know what the tabloids have reported. But do you really know the person? Probably not.

Here's the thing, true worship comes out of knowing God not just knowing about God!

—⚒—

**True worship comes out of knowing God...
not just knowing about God!**

—⚒—

So many people have gotten that mixed up. Please don't hear me wrong. I'm all for going deeper. I'm all for digging into God's word. However, I'm afraid that we've made knowledge *about* God synonymous with simply *knowing* God.

How about another classic worship story? (Really, I have enough I could fill the entire book.) At that same church where we implemented the drums, we used a *connection card* in our programs each week. On that card, you could submit your contact information, RSVP for upcoming events, and inform the pastors of a prayer request. We had one particular individual who submitted the same prayer request every single week.

Where's the reverence?

That was it. That was his prayer request. It was more of a comment than a prayer request. But that would have been awesome to have called him up offering to help him become more reverent in his life.

Obviously, he was using his card to voice his complaint. Now, I would understand his complaint had we spent every Sunday merely serving our own personal needs in that church. But that wasn't our behavior. That wasn't our desire. In fact, our desire was to be extremely reverent before our God.

With a little investigation, we discovered that there was more to the story. You know that there's always more to the story, right? There's always something going on beneath the surface. For this man, we were not singing the songs he wanted us to sing. When we did sing the songs he wanted us to sing, we didn't sing them like he wanted them sung.

In my lack of maturity, I wanted to say *go find another church*.

I bit my tongue.

Here's what I've learned since then. This man's cry for reverence was actually a cry for intimacy. Most people can name a few of their favorite songs. When asked why, most people will begin to share about where they were when they first heard the song, or what they were doing, or who they were with. See, what I've learned is that our favorite songs usually have a memory attached to them.

Here's the question. How can we get beyond our past moments and memories and create new ones? Those memories are good, but we cannot live in them. One of my greatest fears is that you will know about God without truly knowing God on an intimate level.

Question... If God showed up right now and told you that you could wish for one thing, what would be your wish? It could be anything whatsoever. One wish. What would you wish for? (And no wishing for more wishes!) Do you know what David wished for? He says in Psalm 27:4 that if there were only one thing that he could ask of the Lord, this is it. Look at this...

> *One thing I ask of the LORD, this is what I seek: that I may dwell in the house of the LORD all the days of my life, to gaze upon the beauty of the LORD and to seek him in his temple.* (Ps. 27:4)

What Does Intimate Worship With Awe and Abandonment Look like...

If you're still wondering what it looks like to worship intimately with awe and abandonment, allow me to show you some practical examples from the Book of Psalm. One quick stroll through the writings and you'll find all kinds of expressions of worship. Here are just a few...

Shout to God	Dance before Him
Bow down	Tell of His might
Meditate on His truth	Still your heart
Run to Him	Lift your hands
Clash the cymbals	Sing a new song
Clap your hands	Seek his face!

CHAPTER 10

Defeating The Drift: Who You Are As A Follower

I can remember when my daughter was in the second grade having to go in for a parent-teacher conference. She hadn't done anything wrong. It was just one of those standard meetings that has to happen every semester. It was a big classroom full with all the parents, some of their kids, and then all of the 2nd grade teachers. They had 20 minutes to brief us on how school was going and on how the children would be graded.

So, I'm sitting there at a desk clearly not designed for a man over six feet tall and the size of a moose. Ally's sitting right beside me all prim and proper. Mary Poppins would have been so proud. I'm trying my best to pay attention to the teacher's explanation about all of the new Georgia standards. I honestly didn't have a clue what they were talking about.

At one point the teacher said something that made me chuckle. I leaned over to Ally and started to whisper something. Do you know what my very own daughter did to me? She quickly... and I mean quickly... looked up and gave me a look that could have killed. No joke! And then she ssshhh'd me! And do you know how I instantly responded!? I instantly shut my mouth, crossed my arms. and sat straight up in my two foot high chair.

After a minute, something occurred to me. I'M THE DAD HERE! Why am I allowing my 7-year old daughter to pressure me like this? The bully!

Have you ever felt pressured to copy someone? At one point or another, we all find ourselves imitating others. As children, we imitate our parents. I can't tell you how many times my daughter has made a facial expression only to hear Amanda say, *that is so your daughter!* As teenagers we imitate other teens. When Justin Bieber came on the scene every boy on the planet had to have that same comb-over haircut and a hoodie. Our kids watch TV shows and then demand to dress in the same clothes they see in the show. We grow into adults and we still do the same, just with more expensive things. Remember these phrases...

- The only difference between a man and a boy is the price of his toys!
- The apple doesn't fall far from the tree.
- Like father, like son.

We have all, at one point or another, copied our lives, our actions, our words, after someone else. It's just our human nature to imitate others. As a result, the media, along with our own personal friends, may submit us to all kinds of peer pressure, causing us not to make the best of decisions. Rather, they cause us merely to copy everyone else.

When you find yourself in a position, facing peer pressure to do something you know you shouldn't do, to act in a certain way you know you shouldn't act, or to go somewhere you know you shouldn't go, I want you to remember 2 words. That's it, just two words. Can you remember two words? This is extremely easy to say but extremely hard to do. Are you ready? Don't copy-cat... Copy Christ!

Copy <u>CHRIST!</u>

That's it. Don't copy-cat, copy Christ! When you feel the pressure coming upon you to conform and be like everyone else, don't copy-cat, copy Christ! In other words, you are to imitate Christ. You are to mimic Christ. You are to be a Christian chameleon copying Christ! Don't imitate your pastor. Don't just go through all of the rituals and traditions and copy the person next to you. Don't copy anything nor anyone in this world; Copy Christ! Here's what the Apostle Paul has to say about copying Christ...

> *Follow God's example, therefore, as dearly loved children 2 and walk in the way of love, just as Christ loved us and gave himself up for us as a fragrant offering and sacrifice to God.* (Eph. 5:1-2)

You don't have to be alive for very long before you realize that there are all kinds of things in this world that will prevent you from following God's example. For example, the comparison trap.

The Comparison Trap...
It's just a natural instinct to compare yourself. You'll look at yourself in the mirror and then you'll look at someone else and you'll make a comparison. The result of that comparison will be one of two conclusions: either you're better than that person or you're worse. Then you'll take that conclusion and place it on your comparison table.

You have a comparison table, right?

Everyone has one.

A young lady will look at another young lady and compare how pretty she is. A young man will look at another young man and compare how popular he is. Parents will compare themselves to other parents based upon their children's grades, or maybe their behavior. I'm not immune either. You should see the size of guns I'm packing on each of my arms. They're the size of... BB's. How do I know that? Because I've compared them to other guns. Seriously, as a preacher, it's so difficult not to compare myself to other preachers. It's difficult not to compare Christ's Church to other churches.

And here's what you'll do in the midst of those comparisons. You'll step back and you'll either say, *I'm doing pretty good.* Or you'll say, *wow I'm a loser!* The comparison trap will either leave you full of unhealthy pride, or it will leave you empty of all hope.

But the trap goes deeper. Depending on who you compare yourself with, that person will then determine your standard. This is why there are so many people throughout this world who think that since they are good then God must approve of them. How did they come to the conclusion in the first place that they are good? Because they compared themselves to someone not quite as good as themselves. The problem is found in how we define *good*. And for most, *good* is defined as better than others. So many have deceived themselves into thinking that God approves of them simply because they are better than other people.

Paul tells us to follow *God's example* not someone else's example. Rather than copying someone else why not copy Christ?

The Competition Trap...

Sports is a classic example of how powerful competition can be in our lives. Now, before I go on, just let me clarify that I don't really like those sports leagues for young kids where they don't keep score. You know what I'm talking about. When you ask someone why they don't keep score, some soccer mom replies... *Well, all of our kids are winners.* Gag me! That's not real life. Winning and loosing is real life. Learning how to work through loss is real life. (Can you tell I'm little passionate about it?) Competition is the central theme of every sport. The thrill of victory and the agony of defeat. Without competition, sports would not exist.

My wife and I love the olympics. It doesn't matter whether it's the summer olympics or the winter olympics. We've really gotten into the swimming events in years past with the Phelps and Locte rivalry. Gymnastics is another area. I hate to admit it, but when our guys or girls are killing it in gymnastics, I watch. For me, though, my favorite is hockey in the winter olympics. I've been a huge hockey fan for years. Some people will judge me because it's so violent. (I'm convinced more people would watch golf, though, if you could high-stick and slash with the golf club. Just saying!) I love hockey.

One of my favorite stories of all time is the 1980s USA Olympic Hockey Team. I can watch the movie *Miracle* over and over. Every time, when the announcer shouts, *do you believe in miracles,* I have to state back, *as a matter of fact, I do!* But at the end of the day, whoever gets the puck in the net the most goes home with the gold medal. Swim a fraction of a second slower and you won't be standing on the platform. Competition is what sports is based on.

One of the primary things that drives us in this world and especially in our culture is competition. We compare and compete in every way imaginable. The standard by which you compare and compete will determine your level of satisfaction in this life.

Surely there's a better way.

There was a guy in the Old Testament named Solomon. Next to Jesus Christ himself, this guy was labeled as the wisest man to have ever walked the planet. He had more material possessions than anyone else had ever had. He had more gold, more armies, more wives, he had it all. Do you know what he had to say about comparison and competition? Here it is...

> *Then I observed that most people are motivated to success because they envy their neighbors.* (Ecc. 4:4)

Those are very wise words. It places every single one of us in the same boat. It doesn't matter if you were popular growing up or if you were a nerd. It doesn't matter if you're the CEO of a Fortune 500 company or if you work in the mailroom in the basement. It doesn't matter who you are, this applies to every single one of us.

Surely there's a better way than just trying to *keep up with the Jones*.

I've heard it said that all of us are using someone else to look at as our mirror. We're not looking at ourselves in the mirror. We're looking at someone else and then beating ourselves up because we don't look the same. According to what Paul says, you shouldn't be trying to copy someone else, you need to copy Christ!

The Insecurity Trap...

There's one final trap you should be aware of. If you haven't yet noticed, all three of the traps I've listed are intricately tied to one another. Comparison leads to competition. Competition leads to comparison. Both of them lead to insecurity.

Your insecurities will drive you to do things you probably wouldn't normally do. It's the drive to measure up. The drive to be just as good, have just as much, or look just like the next person. At the core of those actions you'll find your insecurities. Allow these words from Peter to encourage you...

> But you are a chosen people, a royal priesthood, a holy nation, God's special possession, that you may declare the praises of him who called you out of darkness into his wonderful light. (1 Pet. 2:9)

I have mentioned throughout this book that you are not a mistake. God knew exactly what He was doing when He created you, and according to what Peter is saying, God *chose* you! Let that sink in for just a moment. The next time you compare yourself to someone else, remember that God chose you. The next time you find yourself stuck in the endless cycle of competition, remember that God chose you. The next time you doubt your importance in this world, remember that God chose you.

When God looks down at you, he doesn't see the flaws that you see. When God looks down on you, he doesn't see your past mistakes. When God looks down at you, he doesn't compare you to someone else. Peter says that you are *God's special possession*. Your identity is not in your appearance. Your identity is not in your marriage. Your identity is not in your workplace or your school. It's not in your past. Your identity is in Christ. And when your identity is in Christ, there is nothing on the face of this planet that can altar *whose* you are!

Love Redefined...

Ask ten different people to define love and you'll get ten different definitions. Several years ago, Oprah chose our town (Kingsland, Georgia) to conduct a *love* experiment. What began as a couples dating show was quickly overhauled when the people in my community didn't show much interest. Suddenly, Oprah and her crew found themselves scrambling for content to make their show come to life.

The name of the show was *Lovetown U.S.A.* While she came at the topic of love from a fairly worldly perspective, we decided at Christ's Church to explain love from God's perspective. That got the attention of the producers of the show. They approached us about taping a Sunday morning service to possibly use throughout the television series.

I welcomed the opportunity. My philosophy was even if they do not use a second of the footage, we still have an opportunity to touch a lot of people through their productions crews.

I got slammed from other churches in the community.

In a city now termed *Lovetown*, their comments were hardly loving. Disguised as holy remarks, it was clearly nothing more than an attempt to compare and compete.

It's sad that churches compare and compete with one another.

It's sad that they find their identity from the world's standards.

Isn't that how the Pharisees lived their lives?

As we began to unpack a biblical definition of love, the starting point had to begin with what we are pursuing most in this life.

Your pursuit in life will dictate what consumes your life...

In other words, if your end goal in life is just to be famous then your life will be consumed with taking steps towards fame. If your end goal is to be rich then you will be consumed with taking steps that will make you money. It makes sense, right? If all you've ever wanted was a Chevy Camaro that looks like Bumble Bee in *The Transformers* movies, then you'll be consumed with getting a job that pays enough money so you can get that specific car.

Like I've said so many times throughout this book, there is nothing wrong with the things listed above. Fame is not a bad thing. Being rich isn't either. I don't know about you, but I'd love to have a yellow Chevy Camaro with black racing stripes. Those things are not inherently bad. If you're not careful, though, you'll begin to find your identity in whatever it is in this life you pursue. That pursuit will consume you rather than being consumed by God.

A couple thousand years ago, when Jesus walked this earth, he had to deal with some folks who thought they should be looked upon as the most prestigious, most respected, most revered people of their day. They weren't pursuing God. Rather they were pursuing a lifestyle where they would gain the attention of man. They continually tried to trap Jesus in His teaching. There's one such example in the Gospel of Mark, chapter 12, that I'd like to share with you...

> *One of the teachers of the law came and heard them debating. Noticing that Jesus had given them a good answer, he asked him, "Of all the commandments, which is the most important?" 29 "The most important one," answered Jesus, "is this: 'Hear, O Israel: The Lord our God, the Lord is one. 30 Love the Lord your God with all your heart and with all your soul and with all your mind and with all your strength.' 31 The second is this: 'Love your neighbor as yourself.' There is no commandment greater than these." (Mark 12:28-31)*

What was Jesus talking about when he said to love God with all your heart, soul, mind and strength? In a nutshell, Jesus was saying that whatever you pursue in life will consume you. The things of this world will consume you. Obtaining more in this life will consume you. However, if you pursue God then God will consume you.

Jesus, in no uncertain terms, states that if you are going to Love God, you can't do it by only submitting a portion of yourself to God. If you are going to be consumed by God, you can't divide yourself up and only offer God a fraction of your life. Do you know what will happen to you if you try to divide up your life and simply offer God a portion of yourself? You will end up a religious schizo!

The Heart Is The Command Center Of The Body...

I had lunch a while back with a man who has struggled for a while to give 100% of himself to God. I totally related to his story. I don't know if you can or not. He told me that he wanted to believe in God's promises. He wanted to believe that God was a good god. That he was a loving, graceful god. And as things flowed along pretty smoothly in his life then he would start down that path towards giving up 100% of himself to God. However, something tragic would happen in his life or in those around him. Of course, we all know that is precisely the time when the Evil One wants to get inside of our heads and hearts and cause us to doubt. A few weeks later, he came forward and gave it all up. He surrendered. He admitted that he wanted to understand why everything that happens in this life happens. But he just wasn't capable.

When you refuse to give up all to God, you'll evolve into a religious schizo.

Religious schizos struggle with their identity!

Jesus says, *God wants your heart*. And not just part of it, all of it! You see, when the Bible speaks about the *heart*, it's not just talking about an organ that simply pumps blood throughout the rest of your body. It's not talking about an organ that simply fuels the rest of your body. It's talking about your command center. The heart is where decisions are made, where dreams are dreamed, and where ideas come to fruition.

Likewise, when the Bible talks about the heart, it is referring to the area that controls our feelings, our emotions, desires, and our passions. The heart is where we either make our commitment to God or we don't. You are either going to pursue God with all of your heart and therefore be *consumed* by God, or you won't.

It's your choice.

What will you pursue?

I know I already addressed the power of money, but this verse applies to so much more than just money in our lives...

For where your treasure is, there your heart will be also. (Matt. 6:21)

Maybe we need a heart check.
Most of us do. Everyday. If for nothing else than to reestablish our identity as children of the Almighty God.

Your Soul Is Your Source Of Motivation...
Have you ever experienced one of those turn-around moments where all of a sudden you have to do something? You can't keep sitting. You can't keep sleeping. A burst of energy has pulsed through your veins and you have to get up. Maybe you had a few too many cups of coffee. Maybe it was indigestion. Maybe it was a second wind while working out. Or, maybe it was your passion emerging.

I'm not an exercise enthusiast by any stretch of the means. I should be. I could stand to lose a few pounds. However, I do occasionally walk a few miles. (Emphasis being on the world *occasionally*.) I believe what I have experienced is relative whether your distance is a mile or a marathon. At some point, you hit a wall. You run out of steam. You run out of breath. You run out of running. You doubt. You think more about Grandma's French toast breakfast at Cracker Barrel than you do making it another mile. (Okay, maybe that's just me.) You hit a wall.

The wall happens in almost every area of our lives. If you've been married for longer than a few years, I'm certain your relationship has hit a wall. If you've gone through the same routine in your workplace day after day, I'm guessing you've hit a wall. In sports it's called a slump. In your personal growth it's called a dry spell. As an author, it's called writer's block. (What would happen if I stopped writing right now?)

Several years ago, I attended a worship conference at the Billy Graham Training Center in the Smokey Mountains. The views were breathtaking. The people serving on campus were a breath of fresh air. The Hillsong team from Sidney, Australia led us in worship and Darlene Zschech was the featured speaker. They were some of my most memorable moments of worship in my entire life.

Throughout her teaching, Darlene talked about the wall. (Yes, we're on a first-name basis. I met her and hugged her!) For her, it was in a couple of areas of her life. She had experienced hitting the wall while trying to write fresh new worship songs, but tied directly to that was the wall she experienced on a personal and spiritual level. I will never forget the point she made.

Yes, when you hit the wall, the wall seems larger than anything you've ever seen before. The wall is tall. The wall is wide. The wall is thick. The wall appears to be an obstruction between you and where you need to go. In that moment, you will make one of three decisions. You can turn around and go back the way you came. You can give up, sit down on the side of the road and have a pity party for yourself. Or, you can begin to chip away at that wall.

There is something that we often fail to realize when we face the wall. So many of us have given up. We turn around. We claim that the wall is just too big. We forget that our Daddy is SO much bigger than that wall. And... Don't miss this... more often than not, what lies on the other side of that wall in your life is the miraculous.

Do you believe in miracles?
As a matter of fact I do!

> **What lies on the other side of that wall
> in your life is the miraculous.**

Together with the heart the soul determines our conduct. It is out of our heart and soul where great things are born. On the flip side, however, the soul is also where evil thoughts and doubt come from. The soul is where you get raw will power to keep chipping away at your wall. When we are commanded to offer all of our soul, the Bible is referring to all of our energies. All of our focus. To be consumed wholly and completely by God.

Music, in general is a perfect example of how powerful our soul can be. I'm sure you've experienced what I'm talking about. If you've ever watched American Idol, then you've heard the difference between someone who sings with soul and then one who does not. Some sing with incredible passion. It floods out of them like a tidal wave. Others, not quite so much. There are those when they sing, I'm not really sure what kind of words to use to explain it. I'm not sure what it is, but I know it wasn't soul. It definitely didn't motivate me. There is something universal that happens when somebody sings with their entire soul, with every ounce of passion within them. It moves you and motivates you.

Your Mind Is The Birthplace Of Opinions...
I believe, or I should say, it is my opinion, that out of all four areas that Jesus mentions in the passage in Mark we read earlier, that for many of us this will be the most difficult. If you're like me, I'm slightly biased towards my own opinions. I'm not exactly sure I'm

ready to give up all of my likes, my dislikes, my preferences, and my opinions to God.

Isn't that the tendency we have? To take what God has to say in His word and mix in a little bit of our own personal opinion. Just enough to make it more comfortable for ourselves. If that's the case then you haven't given *all* of your mind to God.

If you've stepped up to the age of the smartphone, then you know the frustration of having a phone and a computer that aren't synced up. You put in a new contact in your computer, but then when you're out on the road, it's not there on your phone. Or maybe you write yourself a note on your phone while you're out and about, but then you can't find it on your computer. We can send a man to the moon, but we can't make it simple as pie to sync a phone with a computer.

That's exactly what we do when we begin to mix our own opinions with what God has already stated within his word. There is a place for our opinions. In fact, I believe that God welcomes our opinions, but before we press our opinions upon anyone else we must first weigh our opinions upon his word. I believe God wants you to love him not only with your emotions, but also your intellect as well.

I can remember in bible college learning about the three primary influences that are used to determine our identity as followers of Christ. These three areas will determine what you believe and what you choose not to believe. First, there is the bible itself, what it says and what it does not say. If the bible says it, then you can't argue with it.

Second is our logic. God gave you a brain for a reason and he expects you to use it. God doesn't want you just to rinse and repeat what your parents told you was the truth. God wants you to discover that Truth for yourself. Through our logic we determine what makes sense and what does not. As we read the bible, through our logic, we can now begin to understand any deeper meanings by studying things such as the context of the passage. When was it written? Who wrote it and to whom? Why was it written? All of those aspects play into determining the bottom-line truth.

The third area is our emotions. This is the area that gets us confused. For example, even if the Bible did not say *Thou shall not murder,* logically and emotionally, I still know that it's wrong. That's easy to understand. In our day and age, though, we tend to lean upon our feelings more than the Word of God. We'll say things like, *if it feels right then it must be right.*

If you get the priority level of those three areas all mixed up, you'll get your life all mixed up. If you begin to place your feelings above Biblical truths you'll begin to travel off into left field. If you begin to place your logic above the bible, you'll be left wondering who you are in this life. The Apostle Paul says this...

> *Do not conform to the pattern of this world, but be transformed by the renewing of your mind. Then you will be able to test and approve what God's will is—his good, pleasing and perfect will.* (Rom. 12:2)

What does it take to *renew your mind?* I believe the starting point is giving it up to God and allowing who you are as a person to be reflected by him.

Your Strength Produces Action...

When we're instructed to love God with all of our *strength,* I believe that includes three areas of our lives. It includes our time, talents and possessions. Let me clarify that he's not saying you must physically give 100% of those three things to him. Rather, he's asking that you *honor* him with 100%. There's a significant difference.

One of the easiest ways to understand this would be with our money. Obviously, you can't walk into your church and put your entire paycheck in the offering basket. You wouldn't be able to survive till your next payday. God didn't ask for your entire paycheck. God just wants you to honor Him with it. Recognize where your time comes from. Recognize that you have talents because He gave them to you. Recognize that the only reason you get a paycheck is because you have a job which God provided for you.

You see, our love for God should be a response to God's love for us. However, we will never respond to God's love for us if *what* we pursue in this life is consumed with and centered on ourselves. Find your identity in Christ rather than yourself.

I believe once you find your identity in Christ, your response will be all of the above. To give all of your heart, soul, mind and strength. You're not an accident. God intentionally created you. No matter what anyone else may say. You're alive because God has a purpose for your life.

Do you want to stop drifting?

Give him your all.

Heart... Mind... Soul... Strength!

Closing Comments

I hate cats. Well, actually, hate is a relative word. There is hate and then there is *HATE*! So, let me clarify. I *HATE* cats! (See how I waited till the end of the book to share that bit of imperative information?) Seriously, I very much dislike cats. They whine. They're prissy. They think the whole world revolves around them. I just wanna smack 'em! And if you have one of those litter boxes inside of your house, that smell is beyond awful. There is simply nothing I like about cats.

If you own a cat and love them, I respect you. I don't understand you, but I still respect you.

On the other hand, I love dogs. I'm talking manly dogs. Not those small little rodent-size things. I had a full size collie while I was growing up. He looked just like Lassie. (Some of you right now are wondering who Lassie was, huh? Google it.) That collie was an awesome dog. While I was in the Air Force, I had a Siberian Husky. He was a cool dog. He had those ice-blue eyes that would stare right through you like a laser. However, he was extremely stubborn.

After getting married, my wife and I got a Great Pyrenees. Ever seen one? They're like a giant, massive ball of white fur. We lived in Georgia at the time and she loved to roll around in the orange Georgia clay in our yard. So, she wasn't white very long after getting a bath. She weighed in at around 120 pounds. They are nicknamed the "gentle giant" because their size is a little scary, but their temperament is very gentle. She was another great dog that we had.

All dogs go to heaven, right? All cats go to... well, I guess I won't finish that sentence. By far, though, some of the coolest dogs I've ever come across have been pure mutts. I love that pure, 100%, *Heinz 57* breed.

That's what I love about Christ's Church. We're a mutt. We've got a little bit of everyone. We have Catholics and Charismatics and everyone in between. I love that because we refuse to get hung up on the silly, petty things that have caused so many churches to split throughout the years. I love it even more because I believe it's a great image of what heaven will be like. You realize that all kinds of people will be in heaven, right?

—⁂—

You realize that all kinds of people will be in heaven, right?

—⁂—

There will probably be people you never really liked here on earth.

There will probably be some you didn't think would make it to heaven.

I love the fact that there will be all kinds of people in heaven: Every skin color; Every language; Every tribe; Every tongue; Every church denomination. (Ouch! Really?) The Baptists; The Methodists; The Pentecostals; The Lutherans; (Really, there are too many to list.)

Will you be there too?

I hope you will join me.

One of my favorite passages in the bible talks about how God takes our flaws and transforms them into perfections. Even if we feel like a mutt! Paul writes…

> *Therefore, I urge you, brothers and sisters, in view of God's mercy, to offer your bodies as a living sacrifice, holy and pleasing to God—this is your true and proper worship. 2 Do not conform to the pattern of this world, but be transformed by the renewing of your mind. Then you will be able to test and approve what God's will is—his good, pleasing and perfect will. (Rom. 12:1-2)*

We've come full circle from where we began. I'm still sitting at the tip-top point of my cruise boat. As I scan the horizon I can't see any land as far as I can see. However, I can see a couple of other ships. As I watch their position in comparison to ours, they seem very intentional. They're not just floating around. They're not just drifting wherever the current takes them. I'm sure they have a destination where they hope to arrive.

If you've ever been to the beach, you know how powerful the current can be. It can push you to shore. It can pull you out to sea. It can swing you down the coast. In short, the current is more powerful than you alone. Sure, you may be able to swim against the current for a while, but it won't take long before you run out of steam and hit a wall.

You have a destination. Random drifting won't get you there. Only a life of intentionality will. I hope the message of this book has been clear. As I've shared part of my life and as I've been vulnerable with you, I hope you can learn from my drifting mistakes so that you can defeat the drift in your life.

Over the next several pages, I have some challenges for you. If you're just beginning to go deeper in your faith journey, I would not necessarily recommend that you take all of the challenges simultaneously. Rather, take one challenge at a time. Complete one and move on to the next. I'm confident as you intentionally seek God that your energy and efforts will be well worth your time.

Be intentional…

Defeat the drift!

APPENDIX A

The Proverbs Challenge

There are thirty-one chapters in the book of Proverbs. Inside are many of the world's wisest words that have ever been penned. Most of them were written by the world's wisest man, Solomon.

The challenge here is to read the *Proverb Of The Day*. In other words, on the eighth day of the month, you would read Proverbs, chapter 8. That's all. No more. Then on the next day, you'll read Proverbs, chapter 9.

However, I want you to do a little something extra. At the end of your reading, I want you to take a few minutes and note which verse stuck out to you and why. Write down a few sentences that explains why that particular verse jumped out to you today.

It gets really cool if you repeat the Proverbs challenge month after month. You may think it will get old, but here's what will happen. Next month, you'll have a different verse that sticks out to you. Do you know why? Because you'll be going through something different in life. You read exactly the same thing as you did the previous month but God spoke to you in a unique way.

Want to take it to the next level? Take the Proverbs Challenge every month and on this day next year, look back at your journal to see what jumped out at you then in comparison to now. That's called intentionality and it will defeat the drift in your life!

Here's what I want you to do: I want you to get out your favorite Bible translation and turn to the Proverb that corresponds with today's date. Read it and note which verse sticks out to you the most. Finally, write down in a journal which verse spoke to you today and why. The entire daily process shouldn't take you more than a few minutes each day, but the effects will be priceless. Why not start today?

Oh, one final thought. The question is always asked, what do I do if the month doesn't have thirty-one days. Why not use the final couple of days of the month and tackle a couple of extra chapters?

APPENDIX B

The Romans 8 Challenge

I believe the most power-packed chapter in the entire bible is Romans, chapter 8. Have you ever read it? I can remember the first time I did. I walked away thinking I could conquer the entire world. Scale a building in one leap. Fly faster than a speeding bullet. If you've ever doubted the infinite power of God, go read through Romans, chapter 8.

For the sake of keeping this book from becoming the size of a novel, I haven't reprinted the chapter for you. Just look it up in your own Bible. Unlike the Proverbs Challenge, though, I want you to read Romans, chapter 8, over and over. Actually, I want you to read the entire chapter, once per day, for a week. If you really want to take it to another level, read the chapter everyday for a month. Each day, I want you to write down a few thoughts, just like you did with the Proverbs challenge.

Before you start, though, I want to prepare you. Kind of like a coach prepping his team before they take the field. I can tell you exactly what's going to happen, especially if you read it for a month. Remember us talking about the *wall*. Sure, it's a metaphor. But the wall feels very real. Sometime around day five or six, you'll hit the wall. You'll be telling yourself that you get it. After all, you've already read it six days in a row. What's one more time going to do for you? But, I'm telling you, push and push and push through that wall.

If you can persist, swim against the current, defeat the drift, I believe on the other side of that wall, you will experience the miraculous. I'm not saying that you'll be miraculously healed or anything, but I do believe that God will begin to speak to you in ways you've never heard him speak. Keep pushing. Chip away at that wall. Don't give up.

Do you believe in miracles?

As a matter of fact I do.

Ready - Set - Go!

APPENDIX C

Resources For Further Growth

Books:
Not A Fan by Kyle Idleman
The Purpose Driven Life by Rick Warren
Jesus Is _____ by Judah Smith
Celebration Of Discipline by Richard J. Foster

Online Resources:
www.YouVersion.com - Numerous translations of the Bible, free on your phone, tablet and computer.

www.BibleGateway.com - Free Bible and study tools on your computer.

www.ChristsChurchCamden.com/messagearchive - Watch previous messages online.

www.ChristsChurchCamden.com - Find resources to help you take your next step.

Acknowledgements

Thank you to Princess Cruise Line and the Caribbean Princess ship and its crew. I'm sure you didn't realize that you created the perfect environment for me to complete the manuscript for this book. Thank you for not allowing us to *drift* while at sea!

Thank you Al, who worked hours and hours to help me edit this book. I would have never accomplished this without you!

To Mom and Dad, who have always encouraged me to shoot for the sky, thank you for being such Godly parents and for instilling in me the belief that this naive, corn-fed boy from Indiana might just be able to touch the world!

Thank you, Kevin, for your unending encouragement. I wouldn't be the man I am today apart from your mentorship. You always told me that I could write a book. Now it's your turn!

To my best friend, Juan, the craziest *Mexican* I know. I couldn't ask for a better-best friend. Thank you for always having my back!

Thank you to the pastors and staff of Christ's Church Camden (Matt, Juan, Allison, April, Sabrina, Melonie and Wayne). Without you, our church would not be who they are. I couldn't ask for a better staff! It's because of you that we continue to see God move in amazing ways. Many of the stories throughout this book would not exist apart from your dedication to God and your passion for His people.

Thank you to the elders of Christ's Church Camden for continuing to seek God's vision for our church, our community, and even the world. God has truly blessed our church with very wise men!

Finally and most importantly, to my wife, Amanda for your unending support and love. Through the happy times and the painful ones, you have always kept me strong. I couldn't think of a better *first lady* for our church! :) Love you, hon!

Scott Clevenger is the Lead Pastor of Christ's Church Camden (www.ChristsChurchCamden.com), one of the fastest growing independent Christian Churches in America. What began with only eight people has grown to over 1,200 in less than eight years. He holds a master's degree in church leadership and practical ministries, and is currently seeking his doctorate in church culture.

Scott is passionate about coaching pastors nationwide. Out of that passion, he founded Church Culture Guru and writes to pastors frequently on his site, www.churchculture.guru.

Scott, his wife, Amanda, and their daughter live in the Kingsland, Georgia area where Christ's Church Camden began.